PENGUIN BOOKS

GO-GIVERS SELL MORE

'The great upside-down misconception about sales is that it is an effort to get something from others. The truth is that sales at its best – at its most effective – is precisely the opposite: it is about giving.'

With their international bestseller *The Go-Giver*, Bob Burg and John David Mann took the business world by storm, showing that giving is the most fulfilling and effective path to success. That simple, profound story has inspired hundreds of thousands of readers around the world – but some have wondered how its lessons stand up to the tough challenges of everyday real-world business. Now Burg and Mann answer that question in *Go-Givers Sell More*, a practical guide that makes giving the cornerstone of a powerful and effective approach to selling.

Most of us think of sales as convincing potential customers to do something they don't really want to. This mentality sets up an adversarial relationship and makes the sales process much harder than it has to be.

As Burg and Mann demonstrate, it's far more productive (and satisfying) when salespeople think like go-givers. Cultivate a trusting relationship and focus exclusively on creating value for the other person, say the authors, and great results will follow automatically.

Drawing on a wide range of examples of real-life salespeople who have prospered by giving more, Burg and Mann offer tips and strategies that anyone in sales can start applying right away.

Visit www.GoGiversSellMore.com for downloads and other goodies

W9-ANN-873

'Burg and Mann have beautifully captured the highest purpose of business: to add value to other people's lives. *Go-Givers Sell More* is simple, practical, and, above all, amazingly effective – a blueprint for achieving a successful life' Loula Loi Alafoyiannis, President, Euro-American Women's Council

'*Go-Givers Sell More* will not only teach you how to sell more, it will give you wisdom to live a rich and abundant life' Grandmaster Jhoon Rhee, American Tae Kwon Do founding father, martial arts instructor for Bruce Lee and Muhammad Ali

'For those of us who have always thought of sales as a dirty word or necessary evil, Burg and Mann remind us, brilliantly and compassionately, that it really is possible to do well by doing good' Jennifer Kushell, *The New York Times* bestselling co-author, *Secrets of the Young and Successful*

'*Go-Givers Sell More* will radically change how you see business – and make you radically more successful' Cameron Johnson, television personality and international bestselling author, *You Call the Shots*

'This marvellous book gets to the heart of successful selling: a genuine attitude and spirit of connecting with others. You will learn how to open your heart and mind in new ways to improve your sales career' Dr Nido Qubein, President, High Point University, chairman, Great Harvest Bread Co.

'This extraordinary book is designed for anyone who wants to bring authentic value to others. A timeless classic with insightful lessons for business, marriage or friendship' Sarah Miller Caldicott, great-grandniece of Thomas Edison and co-author, *Innovate Like Edison*

'Yes, go-givers *do* sell more, in both good markets and challenging ones. But don't take my word for it; read this book and learn that you don't sacrifice profits by being principle-based – you profit *because* you're principle-based' Frank McKinney, bestselling author, *The Tap*

Bob Burg is a highly sought-after speaker who teaches the principles at the core of *The Go-Giver* to audiences worldwide. A former top sales professional, he is also the author of *Endless Referrals*. He lives in Jupiter, Florida.

John David Mann has been writing about business, leadership, and the laws of success for more than twenty years; he is also the co-author of *The Secret Language of Money*. He lives in Hadley, Massachusetts.

Go-Givers Sell More

Bob Burg and John David Mann

PENGUIN BOOKS

PENGUIN BOOKS

Published by the Penguin Group
Penguin Books Ltd, 80 Strand, London WC2R 0RL, England
Penguin Group (USA), Inc., 375 Hudson Street, New York, New York 10014, USA
Penguin Group (Canada), 90 Eglinton Avenue East, Suite 700, Toronto, Ontario, Canada M4P 2Y3
(a division of Pearson Penguin Canada Inc.)
Penguin Ireland, 25 St Stephen's Green, Dublin 2, Ireland (a division of Penguin Books Ltd)
Penguin Group (Australia), 250 Camberwell Road, Camberwell, Victoria 3124, Australia
(a division of Pearson Australia Group Pty Ltd)
Penguin Books India Pvt Ltd, 11 Community Centre, Panchsheel Park, New Delhi – 110 017, India
Penguin Group (NZ), 67 Apollo Drive, Rosedale, North Shore 0632, New Zealand
(a division of Pearson New Zealand Ltd)
Penguin Books (South Africa) (Pty) Ltd, 24 Sturdee Avenue, Rosebank, Johannesburg 2196, South Africa

Penguin Books Ltd, Registered Offices: 80 Strand, London WC2R 0RL, England

www.penguin.com

First published in the United States of America
by Portfolio, a member of Penguin Group (USA) Inc. 2010
First published in Great Britain by Penguin Books 2010

1

Copyright © Bob Burg and John David Mann, 2010

The moral right of the authors has been asserted

Printed in Great Britain by Clays Ltd, St Ives plc

A CIP catalogue record for this book is available from the British Library

ISBN: 978-0-141-04958-8

www.greenpenguin.co.uk

Penguin Books is committed to a sustainable future
for our business, our readers and our planet.
The book in your hands is made from paper
certified by the Forest Stewardship Council.

To all our faithful readers of The Go-Giver
who have so generously shared our little story
with so many others

CONTENTS

Go-Givers Sell More

Introduction:
The Truth About Selling

"I'm no good at selling!" Have you ever heard someone say that, or perhaps said it yourself? We hear it all the time. Everyone who is not in sales thinks, "I could *never* sell."

Truth is, most people who *are* in sales secretly think the same thing.

There is a reason people feel this way: most of us look at sales *backward*. We may see it as convincing people to do something they don't want to do. But it isn't; it's about learning what people *do* want to do and helping them do that. Or, we may think it's about taking advantage of others—while in fact, it's about giving other people *more* advantage.

But the biggest inversion of all, the great upside-down misconception about sales, is that it is an effort to *get* something from others. The truth is that sales at its best—that is, at its most effective—is precisely the opposite: it is about *giving*.

Selling is giving: giving time, attention, counsel, education, empathy, and *value*. In fact, the word *sell* comes from the Old English word *sellan*, which means—you guessed it—"to give."

This is not how most of us have come to think about

sales. Typically, sales is taught as a set of specific skills, reinforced by a range of techniques, aimed at putting your product into someone else's hands and their dollar into your pocket. From the *prospecting dialogue* and *qualifying questions* to *overcoming objections* and *closing the sale*, every step of the process is mapped out and nailed down. All you have to do, so the idea goes, is thoroughly learn and carefully practice everything in the salesman's bag of tricks, and *you too will become a sales success!*

At least, that's the theory. But it often doesn't work out that way.

Here is the reality: of the hundreds of thousands of entrepreneurs, small business owners, corporate salespeople, independent reps, and others in business who find themselves fulfilling any sort of sales function, *most are having a hard time with sales and selling.*

This difficulty does not typically come from a lack of belief. Most people who are involved in sales genuinely believe in what they're selling. They are excited about the value they can add to other people's lives while making a healthy living for themselves and providing for their families.

But when it comes to the actual selling part? Most of us don't believe we're any good at it. We get performance anxiety or don't feel comfortable with the idea of "pitching." We don't like having things pushed on us, and don't really expect others to like it either.

We want to sell—we just don't want to be in *selling mode.*

If this describes you, even a little bit, then much of what you're about to read may surprise you. The approach in this book may even seem backward compared to what you have learned before about sales. For example:

- Instead of "adding value" *after* the sale or as an incentive to close a difficult deal, our model *starts* with adding value and makes that its principal goal throughout.

- The classic sales process culminates in the "close." Ours focuses on the "open."

- People typically think of sales as a *talking* business. Our approach is to spend less time talking and more time *listening*.

- Conventional sales training focuses on *the presentation*: how you talk about your product. Ours focuses on asking *great questions* and keeping the conversation focused on others.

- The classic sales process succeeds if you "make a sale" and fails if you get a "no." Our sales process starts with the understanding that it is impossible to "make a sale"—yet it is designed so that you will have a positive outcome 100 percent of the time, whether or not a sale happens.

Perhaps the biggest difference in what we describe here has to do with the concept of *control*. The traditional approach to sales, reinforced and fine-tuned by dozens of carefully honed techniques, aims to choreograph the process by putting control firmly in the hands of the salesperson—which is probably why neither party really enjoys it: it's not much fun to have someone try to control you.

For that matter, it's not much fun to be the one doing the controlling, either.

The traditional sales process is typically viewed as a sequence of specific, controlled events:

prospect → qualify → present →
overcome objections → close →
follow up → provide customer service

Go-Givers Sell More takes a different approach. In our view, the sales process goes something like this:

create value → touch people's lives →
build networks → be real → stay open

These five steps correspond to what in *The Go-Giver* we called the Five Laws of Stratospheric Success, which also form the five parts of this book. We'll refer to those five laws often in these pages and even quote the characters from *The Go-Giver*—Pindar, Joe, Nicole, Ernesto, Sam, Debra Davenport, and others.

In fact, this book is based squarely on the premise at the heart of *The Go-Giver*:

Shifting your focus from *getting* to *giving* is not only a nice way to live life and conduct business, but a very *profitable* way as well.

Put another way: living with generosity creates a swelling tide that raises all ships. Not just yours; not just the other person's; *everyone's*.

Being a giving person, as it turns out, is not just an agreeable idea; it's also quite practical. People who grasp and live the principles of giving not only live happier and more fulfilled lives, they are also among the most successful people we know. Go-givers really do sell more.

Now, we have a confession to make: these ideas did not really originate with us. In fact, what we're describing in this book is simply how every truly great salesperson operates.

When you spend time with a genuinely successful salesperson, pay close attention and you'll find something surprising: none of the hundreds of standard sales techniques are what makes them excel at what they do. Oh, they know about them, and when it will serve their customer, they may utilize some of them. But what makes a great salesperson great at sales is that he or she is wholeheartedly interested in *the other person*.

The truth about selling is that it's not about your product, and it's not about you—it's about the other person.

Genuinely great salespeople are not great because they have mastered "the close," or because they give a dazzling presentation, or because they could shoot holes in any customer objection from fifty paces. They are great because they create a vast and spreading sphere of goodwill wherever they go. They enrich, enhance, and add value to people's lives. They make people happier.

But the most remarkable thing about these consummate salespeople is that they are not as rare as you might think. In fact, you can find them everywhere. This is because being adept at sales does not require mastery of complex or elaborate skills. As Debra Davenport says in *The Go-Giver*, "You want people skills? Then be a *person*."

This is very good news, because it means that anyone can be great in sales. It means *you* can be great in sales.

You might think that to do so, you need to have an outgoing, naturally jovial, gregarious personality. Not true. Shy people create relationships and get married. Introverts make great friends. You don't need to be a "people person," or *any* specific type of person, to be great at selling. In fact, the idea itself—that *you* might have to be a certain sort of person to be great in sales—precisely misses the point:

It's not about you; it's about *them*.

If you take away nothing from *Go-Givers Sell More* but those seven words, it will have been worth the effort for us to write it and for you to read it—because your life in sales will transform. Focus on the quality of the relationship and on providing value to the other person, regardless of "making the sale," and you will create an exchange that is both more satisfying *and* more profitable.

That in a nutshell is the message of this book: *it's not about you—it's about them*.

"I loved the story about Pindar and Joe," said one reader of *The Go-Giver*, "and how everything came together at the end of the book. But I can't help wondering, does this stuff really work—I mean, in real life?"

This book is our answer to that question.

It's easy to get distracted by daily headlines and nightly newscasts that focus on the exploits of the well-heeled corrupt in high places. But far from the TV camera's glare, the great majority of genuinely successful people quietly carry on with their lives in ways that bear a surprising resemblance to Pindar, Ernesto, Nicole, and Sam.

But don't take our word for it. Our fondest hope is that as you read *Go-Givers Sell More*, you'll put its ideas to the test and find out for yourself. And as you do, we invite you to share your experiences with our growing Go-Giver community in the Scrapbook section of the Go-Giver blog: www.thegogiver.com/scrapbook.

And not only your experiences with sales. Because *Go-Givers Sell More* is not just about selling more: it's also about *living* more. As Pindar tells Joe in *The Go-Giver*, "These lessons don't apply only to business, Joe. A genuinely sound business principle will apply anywhere in life—in your friendships, in your marriage, *anywhere*."

If you are in sales in any form—as an account exec at a large firm, an independent rep working out of your home, a retail clerk, a professional marketing your own services—then this book is for you.

And if you're not in sales? Then this book is for you, too. It's for anyone and everyone who at any point in the course of everyday life finds themselves dealing with other human beings. Why? Because studying sales is really studying *humanity*. Understanding selling means understanding how people work.

Writing about *The Go-Giver*, one reviewer added this at the end of his column:

7

As a side note, I handed *The Go-Giver* to my thirteen-year-old son and made it a required read. Even if he never touches a sales job or owns his own business, I do believe he will be a much better person because of it.

The five principles explored in this book govern success in sales; they also govern successful friendships and partnerships, marriages and families, and organizations large and small. This is because the laws that govern good salesmanship are the laws that govern good relationships. Selling is not at its core a business transaction; it is first and foremost the forging of a human connection.

If your goal is to make a living through sales, then we'd like to challenge you to set your sights higher. The idea of "making a living" has the sense of breaking even, of keeping your head above water. But you can do more than tread water—why not *soar*?

Most often a goal of keeping your head above water will only end up sinking you. Approaching your work with the attitude, "I hope I make enough to get by" is deadly for sales—because attitudes are contagious. Regardless of what your particular product or service is, people are drawn to you (or not) because of *how you make them feel*. They don't simply want to buy your product, they want to be uplifted, encouraged, changed in some way.

Our purpose in this little book is to help you not simply survive but *thrive*—through your encounters with other people, to enrich their lives on every level, and in so doing, to enrich your own life and the lives of everyone around you as well. The goal is not only to make a good living, but to create a *great life*.

THE FIVE LAWS OF STRATOSPHERIC SUCCESS

THE LAW OF VALUE
*Your true worth is determined by
how much more you give in value than
you take in payment.*

THE LAW OF COMPENSATION
*Your income is determined by
how many people you serve and how well
you serve them.*

THE LAW OF INFLUENCE
*Your influence is determined by
how abundantly you place other
people's interests first.*

THE LAW OF AUTHENTICITY
The most valuable gift you have to offer is yourself.

THE LAW OF RECEPTIVITY
*The key to effective giving is to stay
open to receiving.*

I. The Law of Value

*Your true worth is determined by
how much more you give in value
than you take in payment.*

1. The Law of Value

1. Create Value

I mean, no offense, but how does a hot dog stand manage to out-rank the swanky sidewalk cafés in this neighborhood? —JOE*

If you are hoping to learn how to *make a sale*, we need to make a disclaimer right here and now: in this book we are not going to teach you how to make a sale. We're not going to do this for the simple reason that *you can't* make a sale. No one can. It's impossible to *make* a sale, because you cannot really make other people do what you want them to do.

If you cannot make a sale, then what *can* you do? You can provide the context that allows a sale to happen when the other person makes a purchase. This is not semantics; this is the secret of all great salespeople.

Your job is not to make a sale but to create something else: *value*. In fact, as a salesperson you can define your job description in three words: *I create value*.

*The brief excerpts that open every chapter in this book are all drawn from *The Go-Giver*.

Value is the relative worth or desirability of a thing to the user or beholder. It is those qualities or characteristics in a thing or experience that give it worth, importance, or preciousness—especially as compared to its cost, whether in dollars or other terms.

Four-fifths of selling is creating value. The final one-fifth involves the sale itself; however, even when the sale happens, you don't *make* that sale—you *receive* it. We'll get to the receiving piece of it in part V. For now, let's look at the creating part.

If your goal—as a salesperson or any kind of person—is to create value for other people, how do you do that? There are a thousand ways. Here we'll look at just five: excellence, consistency, attention, empathy, and appreciation.

Excellence

There's nothing like doing what you do well. When you see your work as exchanging hours for dollars, it's easy to slip into a mindset of doing a task just well enough to get by. When you see your work as *creating value*, something shifts.

According to the Law of Value, the point is not to do just enough to get paid, it's to see how much more value you can create than what you are paid for. That translates into *excellence*.

How do you greet people on the phone? How do you manage your correspondence and email? How do you dress? How do you pronounce the other person's name?

You can create value for others by applying the principle of excellence to all the tasks of your trade. If you run a hot dog stand, it means using the best ingredients (never a stale bun, the crispest freshest pickles, only premium all-beef franks), keeping the cart immaculately clean, and keeping yourself that way, too.

The point is not to hold yourself to an impossible standard of perfection. It is to invest yourself consciously in everything you do, with an intention of bringing to bear your greatest abilities to the task at hand. It is to create a habit of excellence.

When you stay at a Ritz-Carlton, you are never greeted with a "Hey," a "What's up?" or a "How ya' doin'?" Depending on the time of day, it will be "Good morning," "Good afternoon," or "Good evening." When you thank an employee for something, the response will not be "No problem" but "My *pleasure*." They say it like they mean it—and they do mean it. Simple. Impressive. What does it cost? Nothing. What does it create? *Excellence*. Any other hotel or motel in the world could do the same thing and position themselves above the competition. But most don't.

Excellent, by the way, does not mean *expensive*. The ability to provide exceptional value is not limited to high-end businesses or those with luxury product lines. You can have a great food experience at an expensive fine dining establishment, a family deli, a neighborhood coffee shop—or a hot dog stand. Price and value are not necessarily the same thing. In fact, when following this law, they *never* are.

Consistency

The world is full of uncertainty. When people know they can always count on you to deliver the same quality of experience, no matter what, you become an oasis of stability within their personal sandstorm of change.

There is a restaurant in John's area that serves pretty good food—sometimes. And sometimes not. John and his wife, Ana, have been there three or four times. There's another place that's about twice as far away and in about the same price range, but their food is *always* good. You can guess where John and Ana eat—and where they don't. It's worth the extra drive not to have to wonder how dinner will turn out.

When you can combine both—excellence plus consistency—you create truly exceptional value.

Attention

Bob uses a travel agent in Florida named Jim Hurlburt. In the Internet age, when we can all make our own reservations, you'd think travel agents would be obsolete—but Bob would never dream of traveling without using Jim's service. Why? Because of the phenomenal value Jim creates through his attention to detail. He gets Bob exactly the flights he wants at the times he wants and for the best prices possible (and saves him a ton of time). He knows Bob's seating preferences, he calls to let him know he got the upgrade—and if he couldn't get it, he'll keep trying till he does. He calls the airline to make sure everything is running on schedule and keeps Bob up to date on any changes.

Before Bob leaves, Jim emails to wish him a good trip and make sure he has Jim's cell phone number in case of emergencies. When Bob returns, there's an email waiting to welcome him home, make sure he had a good trip, and ask if anything came up that would have made the trip easier or better for him.

Not surprisingly, Bob has referred a lot of business his way. The value Jim has created has made him worth a great deal to Bob and has paid Jim back in dividends many times over.

Empathy

Empathy means putting yourself in the other person's shoes.

This is what happened to John and Ana a few years ago when Ana broke her knee. It was a complex fracture and took two full years to heal completely. During that time they traveled a good amount and flew five different airlines, quite a few times each.

When they flew Southwest, Ana was always taken onto the plane first; wheelchairs were always ready for her when they got off the plane; and because she had to keep her leg up for long flights, the flight attendants took care to make sure they got three seats across, with the empty seat in the middle so she could put her leg up—even on flights that were practically full.

Of the other four airlines, none came anywhere close to this level of attentiveness; on one flight they were actually shuffled to the very *back* of the plane. The other airlines gave decent service overall, but they missed so many simple opportunities to add more value. They just didn't get it. They were neither trained nor inclined to put themselves in the passenger's place.

Appreciation

Adding value to people's lives often costs little or nothing financially. In fact, most of the greatest ways we can create value for other people have nothing at all to do with spending money.

One of the most powerful ways you can create value for people is simply to appreciate them. Notice the things they do that make a difference, no matter how small, and point them out. Say thank you, and mean it. Write thank-you notes—not just emails, but actual handwritten notes. (Who does *that* anymore?)

At Marie Jakubiak's accounting firm in Michigan, new clients are not simply greeted by name the first time they walk into the office; they are also greeted by a sign that says, "Welcome to our new client, Mary Jones!" with their name surrounded by fresh flowers.

The word *appreciate* comes from the Latin *appretiare*, which means "to set a price to." Over the centuries it came to mean both "an expression of one's estimate of something, usually favorable" and "to rise in value."

Interesting: when you appreciate people, *you appreciate*. And when you don't, you *depreciate*.

You want to increase your own worth? *Appreciate*.

2. MacGuffin

It was not the hot dogs but the person serving the hot dogs that had vaulted the young man to such popularity. Not the dining— the dining experience. Ernesto had made buying a hot dog into an unforgettable event.

"But I already sell a high-quality product that gives great value," says the skeptic. "My company's got value covered; why can't I just focus on selling my great product?"

Let's say you sell insurance: what business are you in? If you're about to answer, "The insurance business, of course!"—not so fast. It doesn't matter whether you sell cars or homes, legal or financial services, computers or sandwiches: *you're not really in the business of selling any of those things.*

What you sell is a MacGuffin.

A MacGuffin, so dubbed by the late British film director Alfred Hitchcock, is the object around which the whole story focuses. In *Raiders of the Lost Ark*, it is the ancient Ark of the Covenant that the archeologist Indiana Jones is racing to prevent the Nazis from obtaining. In *The Maltese*

Falcon, it is the jewel-studded falcon statuette that triggers multiple murders and betrayals. In *The Treasure of the Sierra Madre*, it is the precious gold hidden in the mountain mine that Humphrey Bogart's Fred C. Dobbs and his partners are desperate to find.

Here's the funny thing, though: when you get to the end of the story you realize, that thing the story's about? *That's not what the story's about*.

Indiana Jones succeeds in his quest, but the ark itself is quietly buried, filed away in a warehouse under lock and key. The Maltese falcon statuette turns out to be a fake. Fred C. Dobbs's gold dust blows away in the breeze. The characters themselves are devoted to their pursuit of the MacGuffin—but the value of the story lies not in the MacGuffin but in the process they go through.

Whatever it is you're selling, *it's a MacGuffin*.

It's not that your product isn't important; it is. It's just not what the sales process is all about.

Then what *is* it about? It's about adding value to the other person's life. Your product may be one vehicle for doing that, one among dozens. Yet a person may never actually buy your product and still have his life changed by meeting you and getting to know you. And that person—even though he never actually becomes a "customer"—will refer many others to you.

You may have been told that the number one ingredient to success in sales is to be head-over-heels in love with your product. After all, how could you get behind something you didn't love passionately yourself?

That idea seems logical, but it isn't.

Would you have to be in love with insurance, software,

or sandwiches in order to sell any of those things, or even be *great* at selling them? No. You *may* be in love with your product, but you don't *have* to be.

You must believe in it. You must back it 100 percent. You must know, beyond the faintest shadow of the slightest doubt, that your MacGuffin will do the job it is supposed to do for the person who buys it. But you don't necessarily have to love it personally.

What you do need to fall in love with—head-over-heels, moonstruck, gaga in love—is the process of helping people get what they need and want. Of *creating value*.

Sometimes being in love with your product can actually get in the way of being great at sales. That passion can come across as a kind of missionary zeal that puts other people off. Accost them with a zealot's gleam in your eye and they'll never hear a word you say. You may care a great deal about your product, but that doesn't mean the other person does, too.

Remember, this process is not about you, and it's not about your product. It's about the other person.

There is very good news here: it means that no matter what you're selling, you have the same opportunity to touch people's lives.

Some will read this and say, "Oh, they're saying the product doesn't matter." We're not saying that at all. The product matters very much. And many great salespeople *are* enthusiastic, committed, lifelong users of their own product, *are* in fact very much in love with their product. But that's not the point.

Your MacGuffin may be the best in its class. It may even be life-changing. You may have testimonials from people who declare that they would never be without your MacGuffin, that they are alive today only because they found out about your MacGuffin. But the MacGuffin is not what the story is about. The story is about adding value to other people by touching their lives.

Danielle Herb was diagnosed with ADD/ADHD when she was just five years old. Unwilling to put her on prescription drugs, Danielle's mother, Marianne, began exploring every way she could think of to support her vision of her daughter being healthy, happy, and fulfilled.

Danielle had always had a passion for horses, and over time the two realized that working with horses was not only something she loved, it was also having a profound impact on her ability to channel her thoughts and attention. It was developing her sense of *self*.

Excited as they were about what they were seeing, they didn't stop there: the daughter-mother team developed a program for other kids to help them learn to communicate more effectively and build their confidence and self-esteem. They founded a private alternative school to help kids who were falling through the cracks of the public school system, and have since developed a spin-off enterprise called Drop Your Reins, a national training and teen mentoring program for kids diagnosed with ADHD or autism.

Drop Your Reins teaches horsemanship—but that is only its MacGuffin. What Danielle and Marianne are really in the business of doing is touching lives.

In *The Go-Giver*, Ernesto built a real estate empire starting with his hot dog stand. His business had nothing to do with hot dogs. Yes, his hot dogs were delicious, but c'mon, they were *hot dogs*—and still he touched people's lives.

3. Giving

When you base your relationships—in business or anywhere else in life—on who owes who what, that's not being a friend. That's being a creditor. —SAM ROSEN

To be successful in sales, it's important to understand how giving actually works.

The essence of the Go-Giver philosophy is this: *the more you give, the more you have.* How can that possibly be true? It seems to fly in the face of logic, and if business isn't logical, then where does that leave us?

But it *is* logical. It just follows a different sort of logic from the one we're used to. It's something like the difference between the classic physics of Newton and the strange world of quantum physics.

Newtonian physics has a 2 + 2 = 4 kind of logic. It is the domain of linear action and response: *every action has an equal and opposite reaction.* Early physics imagined atoms, the ultimate building blocks of nature, as something like billiard balls: inert little balls of matter that move when you hit them, in predictable, linear paths. Pretty simple: bank the 6 ball off the side, hit it into the corner pocket.

Quantum physics discovered that atoms are not inert building blocks at all, but are themselves tiny universes, each embodying unimaginably vast amounts of energy behaving in entirely unpredictable ways that seem to defy Newtonian logic.

Classic business operates by billiard-ball logic: every action has an equal and opposite reaction. You give me a hundred dollars and I'll give you a hundred dollars' worth of lumber. You loan me a thousand dollars and I pay you back a thousand dollars plus interest (that's friction).

Like Newton's laws, billiard-ball accounting works, to an extent. You want to keep your books accurately and pay attention to the balance of income and outgo, payables and receivables. But there's more to business than debits and credits. Billiard-ball logic operates within its circumscribed sphere, but it doesn't govern the interactions of *human relationships*— which are what weave the fabric of all business.

Classic physics says that when you give something away, you no longer have it: transactions deplete. Sell off your lumber, steel, oil, hours, effort, and you deplete your own store. Economics is called the "dismal science" because it catalogs the ongoing process of depletion.

Managing relationships based on the billiard-ball logic of economics isn't very practical, though. It's good for keeping track of widgets, foot-pounds, and minutes on the clock, but not of people and their interactions. We try anyway: "I did the dishes last night; tonight it's your turn." (Every action has an equal and opposite reaction, right?) And for a while, it can seem like it's working—but it never does in the long term. In the effort to keep score accurately, the arithmetic invariably breaks down.

"What most people call win-win," Sam tells Joe in *The Go-Giver*, "is really just a disguised way of keeping track. Making sure we all come out even, that nobody gets the advantage. I scratched your back, so now you owe me."

The secret, says Sam, is to *stop keeping score*.

Managing a relationship with a scorecard doesn't work because nobody can ever measure up to the subjectivity of another's billiard-ball calculations. Millions of marriages have broken up over scorecards that didn't seem (to either party) to tally fairly. Millions of citizens have been conscripted to bear arms in the effort to square warring states' grudge-and-privilege balance sheets. Live by billiard-ball logic, and before long bullets will fly.

Relationships don't work this way because they are governed by an altogether different physics.

Arlin Sorensen is CEO of Heartland Technology Solutions, an information technology company based in Harlan, Iowa. After reading *The Go-Giver*, Arlin organized a Go-Giver–themed summer retreat for his 220-company peer-group organization, Heartland Tech Group, and found a dozen other creative ways to inculcate the idea of *living with generosity* into his business.

In the summer of 2008, as the nation's economy began spiraling downward, Arlin's organization found perhaps its most inspired application of go-giving. Here's how Arlin described it:

This weekend, two of our members took time out from leading their own companies and flew to another state to help a fellow member company who was considering massive layoffs or even closure. After performing a detailed assessment, they were able to provide guidance on immediate action steps to deal with the issues at hand.

I just received their findings-and-feedback report this morning: things for that owner have gone from "futile and overwhelming" to "manageable and possible," and the two members who did the assessment are exploding with additional ideas and suggestions.

Looking back nine months later, Arlin reported on how the situation worked out long-term:

During the fourth quarter, the struggling member was able to regain control of the business, paid off most of their debt, and had enough cash in hand to pay the rest. First quarter '09 was a banner season for sales and profits.

But here is the really interesting thing: the two people who flew out to help the other member's business say they have discovered that *they* have been forever changed by the investment of time, effort, and dollars they made. Not only did they feel personally enriched by the experience, but they also learned much in terms of business acumen, critical thinking skills and leadership—ideas and processes they were then able to bring back and incorporate into growing their own companies.

In the economics of human interaction, spending doesn't deplete, it multiplies. The more knowledge you give, the more you have. The same with appreciation, acknowledgment, wisdom, attention, care. When you keep it to yourself it doesn't build interest; it withers. In fact, the only way you can get more of it is to continuously give it away.

If that sounds familiar, it should: that's not only how giving works, it's also how *love* works. That is the economics of all genuine relationships, and therefore, the dynamic that lies at the heart of sales.

The more you give away, the more you have.

4. Money

"I'm sorry . . . I don't get it," Joe confessed. "That sounds like a recipe for bankruptcy! It's almost like you're trying to avoid making money."

"Not at all," Ernesto waggled one finger. "'Does it make money?' is not a bad question. It's a great question. It's just a bad first question."

Having embraced the importance of creating value, you might be thinking, "Okay, I'm with you so far—but how do I make sure I'm providing value in such a way that it leads to a sale?"

You don't. The task here is not to create value in order to create a sale or "in order to" anything. It's to create value, period.

For you to be a successful salesperson, yes, sales need to happen. They will. But set aside for the moment the idea of "the sale." Right now, your total job is to focus on one thing and one thing only: providing value to other people. If you do that well, sales—and money—will find you.

Money is an echo of value. It is the thunder to value's lightning. Create value, and money follows—it has to. But it's crucial to keep money in its right perspective. As Ernesto puts it, "Does it make money?" is not a bad question; in fact, it's a *great* question. It's just a bad *first* question.

"The first question," Ernesto adds, "should be, 'Does it serve?' or 'Does it add value to others?' If the answer to that question is yes, *then* you can go ahead and ask, 'Does it make money?'"

If putting money first doesn't work, neither does denying money or pretending it doesn't exist.

Have you ever heard people say, "I'm not doing this for the money," as though they were almost embarrassed or apologetic about what they were charging, or as if money itself were not a topic of polite conversation?

What's interesting is that when you have money in clear perspective—in other words, when you *really aren't* doing it just for the money—you won't feel like you have to say so out loud. (Just as genuinely trustworthy people rarely start a sentence by saying "Trust me . . .")

Many of us have a conflicted relationship with money; in fact, it is remarkable how often people sabotage their own success because of the uneasiness of that relationship. There is an assumption, often unspoken, that there exists a fundamental contradiction between self-interest and altruism. That is, you may be acting for others' benefit, or for your own—*but not both at once*. If you accept this treacherous dichotomy, then every time you pick up the phone or walk across a room to talk with a prospective customer, your subconscious has to conclude either:

a) I am greedy, manipulative, and focused purely on my own personal gain at this person's expense—*or*

b) I am big-hearted and generous, on a mission to serve this person, and therefore must deny my own interests and avoid any hint of a result that could actually benefit me.

But this is a false dilemma. Not only are self-interest and altruism *not* in conflict, but in fact, they are two sides of the same coin.

Having a giving spirit does not mean having a spirit of self-sacrifice or martyrdom. The martyr still sees the dualism between helping oneself and helping others, viewing these two as being in conflict. That's not generosity: that's just being a card-carrying codependent. *The true giver sees no such conflict*. The true giver knows that giving is a tide that raises all ships, and that it allows you to be a person of value to others while doing very well for yourself.

James P. Smith, a regional sales director for a marketing services company, was handed a copy of *The Go-Giver* just before boarding a plane in Salt Lake City after giving what he felt had been the *perfect* sales presentation.

I'd had everyone in the room on my side and all agreeing to what I was selling. It could not have gone better, and as I walked out of the meeting I was already counting the money—until I boarded my plane, buckled into my seat, and started reading *The Go-Giver*.

As I turned the pages, I realized that my motivation had been all wrong. I decided right then and there that I had to stop "selling" and start looking at things from the customer's point of view. By the time I landed in Houston I had finished the book and read it through a second time—and was nearly in tears.

Shortly after he arrived home, James received a call from the Salt Lake City company's national marketing director, asking if he could do a specific task.

The obvious answer would have been, "Yes sir, we can," but something in your book made me realize that I knew a better way that was *not* from my own company. I explained that since we were still in beta-test mode with the service he wanted, I would refer him to a company that had it up and running and was better equipped to handle his situation.

The man was speechless. As I hung up an intense satisfaction came over me like never before.

Later, he called back to thank me again for my referral and for my candid honesty, and to say that I could count on a long-term partnership. And that partnership has significantly profited our company.

In sales, an excellent way to keep money in perspective is to create the habit of looking at it from the other person's point of view. How can you provide value for *them*? How can you make sure you're watching out for *their* financial interests? How can you help them increase their earnings and build *their* net worth?

The degree to which you focus on adding value to others, constantly and consistently, will determine your worth, both in the heart and in the marketplace. More value will translate into more positive relationships, a greater sense of self-worth, a greater appreciation of life—and yes, more income.

A few weeks after *The Go-Giver* came out, it was reviewed by Simon Barrett, editor of Blogger News Network. After a few paragraphs of review, Simon added:

> The ideas the authors are suggesting pretty much mirror my own story. About eighteen months ago I decided that I had had enough "fun" in the computer industry. After thirty-plus years I was burned out; I wanted to write. Of course, no one wants to publish or even entertain a new writer. My solution was to "give greater value": I wrote *for free*.
>
> It wasn't long before I started to get invites to write for money. I have not given up my day job, but I am well on my way to doing so.

We checked in with Simon a year later to see how things were going. He had indeed left his day job, and he and his wife, Jan, were now supporting themselves full time with writing and interviews. As Simon put it:

> Once the freight train starts running, things happen. CNN is using us as a source. People I never dreamed would talk to me now come to me. The one thing we are sure about is, if you really want to do something, *you can*. Life is what you make of it.

Once the freight train starts running, things happen. Beautifully said. And the way you set that freight train in motion is by creating value.

5. The Paradox

"Wait," said Joe. "So, 'profitable things begin to happen'—but I thought you said you're not thinking about the results."

"That's right," Ernesto agreed, "you're not. But that doesn't mean they won't happen!"

None of us are saints; we're all ultimately driven by self-interest. Trying to eliminate our sense of self-interest would be a futile effort. Self-interest is an essential part of human nature; it's hardwired. And it's a good thing it is: physiological self-interest is what keeps our heart pumping and our metabolism functioning.

So, does that mean being a Go-Giver is acting against your own nature? Not at all. We don't *need* to erase all thoughts of personal gain to put the Five Laws of Stratospheric Success into effect. All we need to do is place these thoughts to the side for a moment, exercising what British networking expert Thomas Power calls "the willing suspension of self-interest."

We do something similar every time we watch a good film. We *know* it's just a movie; we *know* that James Bond isn't really blowing up an entire terrorist's compound, and that when the lead terrorist points a gun at Bond's head and he responds by coolly cracking a joke, the actor's life isn't actually in danger. But in order to enjoy the story, we *willingly suspend our disbelief.*

When we step into the theater, we make believe that what's up on the screen is really happening so that we can experience the thrill, the fear, the suspense and resolution, the full emotional intensity of the situation, and then bring our sense of catharsis with us out of the theater. We still *know* it isn't real. But by temporarily setting that understanding to the side, we gain emotional access to the entire experience, and even after the film is over and we allow our disbelief to return, we continue to enjoy the effect of that experience.

This is exactly what we do in sales: we willingly suspend our self-interest. We don't erase or deny it; we simply set it aside for a moment so we can gain emotional access to the full experience of the Law of Value.

After reading *The Go-Giver*, blogger Mark Beckford wrote to us to share this experience:

A friend of mine had just opened his own business recruiting attorneys in China. Because I had read your book, my mind went to the thought, "What can I do to help him?"

I realized that an attorney I had worked with was a Chinese national who worked at a law firm in Washington, DC, but split his time between DC and Beijing. I figured he had a great attorney network in China *and* in the U.S. and would be a great contact for my friend.

I introduced the two of them—and my friend then turned into a personal recruiter for *me*, introducing me to more than fifteen new connections.

People sometimes misunderstand this idea and see it as "giving to get." That's not exactly what we're talking about. Giving in order to get is still acting with the *get* in mind—with *getting* as the whole purpose of the exercise. That's something like saying, "Maybe if I act nice, they'll like me and end up buying my product." While this strategy may have the happy result of nicer behavior, it is still behavior that stems from asking, "Will it make money?" as one's first question.

The point is not to act generously *in order to* create a strategic result; it is to act generously, period.

You're not putting others' interests first as a stepping stone toward serving your own interests; you're doing it for the self-contained reward and satisfaction of knowing you were able to serve. You give because it's *who you are* and therefore *what you do*.

"And when you do," as Ernesto says, "very profitable things start to happen."

It's a paradox. If you go about creating value for others with the ulterior motive of receiving more value yourself, it tends to show through on some level and sabotage the result. What Ernesto is suggesting is that instead, you give without emotional attachment to the return—knowing full well that there *will* be return.

6. Your Economy

In fact, Joe, you'd be amazed at just how much you have to do with what happens to you.
— PINDAR

At this point, the skeptic is raising his hand again. "All this giving stuff is all very well," he says, "when times are good and everything is plentiful. But what about when times are bad? Don't we need to take more drastic steps to survive?"

Actually, it's *especially* when times are tough that Go-Giver principles shine.

When the economy goes into a tailspin it's easy to slip into panic mode. But just because economic conditions are always rising and falling, that doesn't mean your own personal economic condition has to rise and fall with them. You are not at the mercy of forces beyond your control. During down times you cannot only hold your own but even get farther ahead.

How? By sharpening your focus like a laser. Your focus on what? On creating value. By creating value for others, you make *yourself* so valuable to the market around you that the demand for you and your business rises even when demand everywhere else is falling.

There is something quite utilitarian about the Law of Value. Its pragmatic beauty is that it places the principal determinant of your success squarely in your own hands, rather than letting it be a factor of your circumstances. While you cannot control what others do, you can control what *you* do. If your goal is to *make the sale*, then you are dependent on the buying decisions of others. But if your goal is to *create value for others*, you are dependent on nobody but yourself.

In fact, here's the remarkable thing about it: when you follow the Five Laws, *you create your own economy.*

Of course you still live in the context of society. Do economic conditions at large still affect you? Sure they do. But they don't dictate the course of your life. You stand on the shore, the tide ebbing and flowing, the surf running over your feet and tugging at your legs. But you have a choice: you can plant yourself solidly on your own moorings, or simply go with the tide like the rest of the driftwood.

So practically speaking, what do you actually *do*?

First, decide that regardless of what's going on around you, *your* economic climate is excellent.

We're not suggesting you live in denial; hard times are hard times. But realize that the flux of human economies is to an extraordinary extent *a state of mind*. The condition of your personal market is largely up to you.

Again, attitudes are contagious. During tougher economic times, people are naturally more cautious and resistant in their buying decisions. Salespeople tend to feel more anxiety, desperation, and panic than in boom times. Intentionally or not, these feelings communicate—and serve to dampen prospective sales even further.

But as a Go-Giver, your attitude is different. Having made the decision to thrive, you can separate yourself from the desperadoes and communicate the fact (whether in words or in pure attitude) that business is fine—*great*, in fact. Adopt within yourself a sense of economic boom times, and let that sense show.

Second, decide you will only intensify your efforts to create value for others.

Providing more in value than you receive in payment is the trade secret of all exceptional businesses. This creates genuine worth that remains bankable in *any* economic climate.

During "down times," most people slow their activities and put the brakes on providing value to the marketplace. But not you. You steadfastly continue on, finding ever new ways to create more value than you take in payment. And by so doing at a time when value seems to be catastrophically shrinking everywhere, you stand out even more than you would in more robust times.

How ironic: for all those whose operational strategy is based on *getting*, an economic slowdown can cripple their businesses, while yours—based as it is on *giving*—remains unaffected and even thrives.

In the fall of 2008, Heather Battaglia was a director and vice president at CitiMortgage, in charge of a very successful and profitable division that she saw as recession-proof. Just before the end of the year, as the economy tanked, she was laid off.

Heather thought she would have no trouble finding a new job. She had strong academic credentials and an impressive résumé of corporate experience. But as she began going through her connections, cold calling, and doing whatever else she could think of to find her new position, no job materialized. A month went by, then two, then three.

"I had never been unemployed before," Heather told us, "recruiters were always finding *me*." Now nothing was working.

Eventually Heather got together with seven other laid-off executives who all belonged to a networking group and created an event for executives who were looking for work. As Heather describes it:

A couple of people in the group had your book, and they said, "Whatever we do for our event, we need to make sure we are helping others and giving first." Here we were, all out of work—and our conversation revolved around how we could help *others* find jobs!

The newly formed ExecNet of St. Louis adopted a mission statement and a vetting process for new members that included the question, "Are you committed to helping other executives first?" In the spring of 2009 Heather reported:

We have over 150 members in our group now—and we're all focused on helping each other first. Many of our group have landed new jobs, others are in final stages of interviews, and others are just getting started. Our group is *only three months old* and we're moving mountains.

Heather and her colleagues were in dire straights. But instead of giving in to recessionary anxiety, they took control of their own state of mind. In focusing their efforts on providing value to others, they created their own booming economy—and it paid off handsomely.

II. The Law of Compensation

*Your income is determined by
how many people you serve
and how well you serve them.*

7. Touch Lives

You know, I always thought it seemed so unfair . . . how movie stars and top athletes pulled down those huge salaries. . . . while people who were doing such great work, such noble work—like schoolteachers—never got paid what they're worth. —JOE

No fair! If you're a parent, you've heard this strident mantra many times. Grown-ups say it, too. *No fair!* is the universal human code for "I don't understand; why should it be this way?!"

For example: isn't it unfair how much our society pays rock stars, sports stars, and movie stars, while the unsung heroes and heroines of our world, the ordinary people, the schoolteachers, beat cops, nurses, and firefighters, are so grossly underpaid?

And what about struggling and mid-income salespeople who have studied just as hard, know their product just as well, and work just as industriously to serve their clients as do wealthier salespeople? *No fair!*

Compensation can seem so arbitrary, can't it? But it isn't

arbitrary at all, and once you understand its governing laws it makes perfect sense.

Most of us were taught that the way to get things in life was to follow this simple three-step program:

- First, aspire to a worthy goal.
- Then, work hard.
- Meanwhile, be a good person.

The key to getting more of what you want, says this paradigm, is simply to do all this *more*. Don't just want something, want it *real bad*. Don't just work toward it, work *real hard*. And while you're doing this, don't just be good, try *really hard* to be a *really good* person.

It all seemed to make so much sense, and we kept following that formula because, by gosh, it *ought* to work. But it doesn't. Don't get us wrong: worthy goals, hard work, and being a good person—these are all fine and necessary pursuits. They're just not in and of themselves the keys to greater success.

Your compensation is not a reflection of your goodness, worthiness, merit, or industriousness: it is an echo of *impact*.

The first law—creating more value than you take in payment—is the bedrock of sales success, but simply creating value for people won't necessarily increase your sales or your cash flow. The second law says that in addition to adding value to the process, you must also *touch as many people's lives* as possible with that added value.

In *The Go-Giver*, Nicole Martin, the schoolteacher-turned-entrepreneur, explains it to Joe this way:

The first law determines how *valuable* you are; that is, it describes your *potential* success—how much you *could* earn. But it's the second law that determines how much you actually *do* earn. . . . To put it another way, *your compensation is directly proportional to how many lives you touch*.

The second law means that a big part of your job is to continually find more people to meet. In traditional sales training, this is called a *funnel* or *pipeline*, as in, "keeping your pipeline full." But this is not the pure numbers game those terms might imply. The question is, what is that funnel made out of? What is its substance? Its substance is *personal impact*.

This is why word of mouth is universally acknowledged as the most powerful and effective marketing force there is.

From Hollywood executives gambling hundreds of millions on the latest summer blockbuster, to a daycare center owner hoping to fill her capacity of a few dozen clients, everyone in business knows that their trade ultimately rises or falls on the quality of the word of mouth it generates. It's not that other forms of advertising and marketing are not effective; they are—but only to the degree that they emulate or reinforce the effect of word of mouth: human beings communicating the impact that an experience has had on them.

Like Nicole, our friend Annette Kraveck started out as a schoolteacher. To help make ends meet, Annette started her own tutoring service. She is a sweet and incredibly patient person, and her kids loved her. Word got around.

Demand for Annette's services grew beyond her ability to provide them, so she began contracting with other tutors to handle the overflow. Before long she was doing quite well financially—far better than she could have done within a school system.

Annette leveraged her value by expanding her reach, which resulted in a dramatic increase in her income.

Although she would not have described herself this way, Annette was *in sales*. What she sold (her MacGuffin) was tutoring services. The reason she came to touch so many lives was not her closing skills (she would say she has none) or a brilliant sales presentation (which didn't really exist) but the tremendous value she created for her kids. The impact she had on those first few students, and the word of mouth it created from parent to parent, is what created her "funnel."

And that is exactly your task: not simply to sell your product, but to create an experience of value that has a positive impact on others' lives.

Money is not a measure of goodness or worthiness. It is a measure of impact. You want more income? Have more impact.

8. People

You want great people skills? Then be a person.

—DEBRA DAVENPORT

Your income, says the second law, is directly proportional to how many people you serve and how well you serve them. Notice the wording: not how many *prospects*, not how many *customers*—how many *people*.

In sales, the people we hope may become customers are usually referred to as *prospects*. It's not a bad word, but it can easily point our thinking in the wrong direction.

The word *prospect* comes from the Latin *prospicere*, meaning "to look off into the distance." It suggests a combination of aspiration and anticipation, hope and intention. In the mid-1800s it became wedded to the idea of panning for gold, and the California Gold Rush's grizzle-bearded prospector was born. This is the context in which the potential sales target—the *prospective* customer—came to be called "a prospect," as in:

"Say, there's Jack Davis; he's a good prospect—let's go

shake him in a pan. Who knows, maybe he'll turn out to contain some gold nuggets there underneath all that mud and silt."

But you're not sifting people to pan for gold here; you're looking for ways to touch lives.

There is no such thing as a "prospect" in real life. It is a concept that exists only in the salesperson's mind, and the more it exists in your mind, the more it can crowd out thoughts of the actual flesh-and-blood person standing in front of you. *Making sales* is a concept. *Touching lives* is a reality. Sales is not about concepts; it's about people.

The dictionary says a prospect is "the possibility, likelihood or mental image of a future event." As long as you're seeing someone as *the possibility of a future event*, you're not seeing the *person*.

Of course you are indeed looking for prospects—but we need to be clear on what we really mean by that. With each new person you meet, you are asking yourself:

"What are the prospects of my touching this person's life?"

Svetlana Kim arrived in New York City in 1991, a refugee from the collapsing Soviet Union, speaking not a word of English and with exactly one dollar in her pocket. She began carving out her new life by looking for ways to add value to people's lives in any small way she could. She began cleaning houses, then sold makeup at a department store, and before long had worked her way up to becoming a very successful financial advisor.

In 2006 she moved to Washington, DC, to work for the Public Affairs Group, one of the most prestigious PR firms in the city.

I was excited—until I discovered that I had to raise $632,000 in nine months! I decided that I was *not* selling stocks and bonds; I was selling memberships and corporate sponsorships—an opportunity to care.

Attending a conference for diversity and leadership, Svetlana happened to meet Loula Loi Alafoyiannis, founder of the Euro-American Women's Council.

I remember our first conversation: short, sweet, and to the point. Loula introduced herself and said to me in Russian, "My name is Loula. I speak fluent Russian. Be in touch."

Svetlana kept in contact scrupulously, never missing a single event at which Loula appeared. She sent her thank-you notes and photographs, returned all her telephone calls promptly, even called her when she was sick to make sure she was doing okay.

I let Loula know that she was important to me, not only as a client but as a *person*. After a while, she began introducing me to her friends and referring clients to me. Before long I had not simply reached my goal but had exceeded it by $300,000.

Bringing in nearly a million dollars worth of business, Svetlana became the number two top producer in her company in less than a year. "And even more important," adds Svetlana, "Loula and I are best friends forever."

Touching a lot of lives means meeting a lot of people.

You will only meet a lot of people if you genuinely want to. And the only way you will be successful at touching their lives is if you become comfortable being with them—not presenting to them or "sorting and qualifying" them, but simply *being* with them. Being great at sales does not take exceptional verbal ability or an extroverted personality. What it does take is the desire to get to know people and the ability to become comfortable being with people.

"But wait," you might be wondering, "how do I know if they'll be interested in my product?"

You don't, and you don't need to. That's not what you're doing here. You're not meeting people in order to make them customers. You're meeting people because they're people and you're interested in their lives.

Some of these people will turn out to be interested in your product or service; others will become excellent sources of referrals. But let's let those results unfold in their own time. Let's make sure we put the cart where it belongs: *after* the horse.

The point here is not to *sell as much product* as possible, nor is it to sell product *to as many people* as possible. It is to *touch as many lives* as possible. The sales and referrals that result are simply a by-product: the thunder to that lightning, the effect to that cause.

9. Rapport

"I've always been good at remembering kids' names," Ernesto explained.

"And remembering their birthdays," continued Pindar. "And their favorite colors, and their favorite cartoon heroes, and their best friends' names." He glanced at Joe and gave the next word emphasis: "Etcetera."

Pop quiz: when you hear the term "typical salesman," what is the first adjective that comes to mind?

When we ask audiences this question, people sometimes say *slick*, or *high-powered*, or *used-car*. But far and away the most common answer is the term *fast-talking*. "It-slices-and-dices-and-squeezes-and-tweezes-and-makes-julienne-fries—*but-wait-there's-more!*"

Why do salespeople traditionally talk so fast? To squeeze in more information. But information is not what makes great sales; what makes great sales is the impact that occurs when you touch people's lives. Contrary to common belief, the "gift of gab" does not make a great salesperson. In fact, those who prattle on typically make the *least* effective communicators, because they shut down the other person and make genuine conversation impossible.

What makes a great salesperson is his or her ability to create a bond with other people. A great conversation is one in which you find points of common interest, gracefully forge a bond through those interests, and allow the *other* person to shine. There is a word for that strong sense of harmonious accord: *rapport*.

If your income is directly tied to how many people you serve and how well you serve them, then knowing how to establish rapport with others is the linchpin to your economic future.

Establishing rapport is not an inborn gift, it is a skill that anyone can develop—and it's well worth doing, even if you never spend a day in a traditional sales job. The ability to create rapport with another is one of the most fundamental skills of being human. It makes life richer.

Building rapport is the opposite of focusing on our differences.

The reason new acquaintances so commonly talk about the weather is that it is something they are both experiencing. That's the essence of rapport: finding common experience. This is why stand-up comedians interrupt their own act to say things like, "Anyone here tonight from Jersey?" They're evoking a common bond. That's why we love discovering that someone we just met went to the same high school, shares the same hobby, has kids the same age, or listens to the same bands.

People *love* talking about their families—their talented spouse, their smart or athletic children. However, there's a pitfall to watch out for here, because you feel the same about *your* family, too, and may feel an impulse to one-up your new acquaintance.

When you ask about someone's family and they swell with pride and mention that they have a daughter who got straight A's in every class this year, it is not helpful to blurt out, "I know what you mean—*my* daughter was on the honor roll. In fact, she's valedictorian, and her teachers are very, very positive about her prospects for early admission to Harvard!"

Look for common ground, but don't let that common ground become a detour into *your* story. This isn't about you.

And what if they tell you about their amazing fourteen-year-old daughter, and you don't have a fourteen-year-old daughter—or for that matter, any kids at all? Not a problem. You might say, "Wow—fourteen, what an age. Remember when we were fourteen?" And he will grin and nod, because of course he remembers. We all do. We're all part of the same human family.

The classic sales formula for a rapport-building conversation is F-O-R-M, which stands for Family, Occupation, Recreation, and Message, the idea being that touching on these particular topics in a conversation is likely to turn up a common interest. Sales training often involves more sophisticated systems for establishing rapport, too, such as neurolinguistic programming (NLP) or the many variations of the "four personality types" (extrovert, amiable, analytical, and pragmatic).

Such teachings offer fascinating insights, and it is certainly worthwhile to become familiar with them. But building rapport does not take the skills of an investigative journalist or master psychologist. Remember, the person you are trying to get to know is a *human being* just like you. The simplest way to establish rapport is to smile. Not too sophisticated, we know, but it's the single most powerful path to rapport ever invented. Here are a few others:

- Be polite.
- Don't interrupt.
- Listen.
- Smile (again).
- Say please and thank you.
- Be genuinely interested in the other person.

As a young girl, Terri Murphy sold Girl Scout cookies. As an adult in Chicago, she regularly sold more than one hundred homes a year. "I've always been fascinated by the prospect of making people comfortable in any situation," says Terri, "and one thing I've learned is that even the biggest barriers will soften and often dissolve when you build even the tiniest bit of rapport."

Terri describes one such situation when she and her husband were going through Los Angeles airport on their way to Hawaii for one of Terri's speaking engagements.

After waiting in line for over an hour to get through, we took our tickets to the Delta Crown Room passenger lounge to get our boarding passes. The woman at the desk studied our tickets for a minute and then said, "I'm sorry, your tickets are not in order—you'll have to return to the main terminal to get the issue resolved."

My husband and I knew that if we had to come back through those long lines again, we might miss our flight. In his most amiable Southern-style courtesy, my husband tried his best to persuade her to "see what she could do," but she was adamant.

We turned to leave—and then something made me turn back for a moment.

Now, I am no linguist, but I come from a big Italian family, and I remember how tough it was for my family when they first arrived in the United States, and the impatience of people in our neighborhood with their limited English. When speaking with foreigners, I love to ask them how to say thank you in their native tongue. Gratitude is one of my core values, and this is a fun way to connect with people and honor their culture.

The woman who did our dry cleaning was Korean and spoke very little English. Every time I dropped off our clothes she would smile and attempt to say "Grazie!" with just the right roll of the r—and I would do my best not to mangle my Korean reply: "Kam'sa'hap'nida!" It would make us both laugh, every time.

At the LAX Delta lounge, while my husband had been talking to our immovable attendant, I had noticed her name tag. It said she was from South Korea. I could at least try to brighten her day a tiny bit, even if she couldn't help us.

I smiled at the woman and said, "Kam'sa'hap'nida." I turned back again and we began walking out of the lounge—and then heard her say, "Excuse me." We turned back and looked at her. "Please," she said, "take a seat over here . . . and I'll see what I can do."

Given Terri's love of people and wonderfully honed sense of rapport, is it any wonder that she made a fortune in real estate, earning her the nickname "the Fourteen-Million-Dollar Woman"?

Milton H. Erickson, one of the greatest figures in modern psychotherapy, was a master of rapport. (In fact, the rapport-based approach of NLP was developed in part through detailed observation of his sessions.) He was also a great raconteur who loved to tell stories about growing up on his family's Wisconsin farm.

As a young man, Erickson sold books to pay his way through college. One day he paid a sales call on a crusty old farmer who was busy feeding his hogs. The farmer had not the slightest interest in the young man's wares and told him to be on his way. As they spoke, Erickson absentmindedly picked up a stray bit of shingle and started scratching the hogs' backs.

The next moment, to Erickson's astonishment, the farmer changed his mind and decided to buy his books—because, he explained, "You know how to scratch hogs."*

Rapport can be as subtle as honoring a person's native tongue, or as simple as scratching a hog's back. It's about being human.

---

*Recounted in Dr. Lynn Hoffman's foreword to *My Voice Will Go With You: The Teaching Tales of Milton H. Erickson*, collected and edited by Sidney Rosen, M.D. (W. W. Norton & Co., 1991).

10. Skills

As long as you're trying to be someone else, or putting on some act
or behavior someone else taught you, you have no possibility of
truly reaching people.   —DEBRA DAVENPORT

Are you sometimes intimidated by the idea of selling? We
understand how you feel. We used to feel the same way,
but here's what we found . . .

You probably recognize the formula embedded in that
last paragraph: it's the famous *feel-felt-found*, one of the
most common arrows in the salesperson's quiver. Feel-felt-
found ("I know how you feel, I've felt the same way myself,
but here's what I found . . ."), the trial close ("If you *were*
going to buy this, what color would you want it in?"), and
the thousand other little tips, tricks, and techniques we
are taught in sales—they can all be useful in their time and
place. Sometimes, though, they can just get in the way.

It's not that skills aren't valuable; they are. There are
many skills you can cultivate to the great benefit of both
yourself and the people you meet. The problem occurs

when using a technique or formula distracts your attention from where it needs to be: on the other person.

To the degree that a skill or technique makes you think about what you're doing, it creates separation between you and the other person. This is why sales techniques can so readily create discomfort: they tend to be me-focused, not you-focused.

Of course, skills can become second nature if you practice them long enough. Like playing the violin, flying a plane, or performing heart surgery, they feel completely natural and work beautifully in the hands of someone who is thoroughly practiced. But most of us will never put in the years of brutal daily discipline it takes to become concert violinists, commercial pilots, or heart surgeons.

Fortunately, sales is not heart surgery. It is a good deal more like dating or making new friends. It doesn't take years and years to master the basic skills. (And if you flop a few times, nobody will die on the operating table.) "Reaching any goal you set," says Debra Davenport in *The Go-Giver*, "takes ten percent specific knowledge or technical skills—ten percent, *max*. The other ninety-plus percent is *people* skills." And developing good people skills is not rocket science.

Many classically taught sales techniques do have a foundation in genuine empathy. For example, the idea behind the feel-felt-found formula is a noble one: it is a way of honoring the other person's experience and feelings. But it easily becomes a rote technique. When you use it that way the other person will usually feel *techniqued*, and whatever rapport you have will evaporate.

One way to keep such skills from becoming artificial is to

make a habit of asking yourself, "What is the truth, right here and now?" For example, before you open your mouth to say, "Yeah, I know how you feel," ask yourself, *do* you really know how they feel? And have you genuinely felt that same way yourself? Too often, the *feel* and *felt* parts of the equation are a mere preamble, a token simpatico gesture offered up in order to get us to the juicy part where we get to talk about *our* experience and knowledge, the "here's what I've found" part. In other words, me, me, me.

Sometimes it can be far more honest to say,

Wow, that must have been painful; I can only imagine how you must feel. I don't know if I can say I've ever felt exactly like that. So, what did you do?

Listening to the person and responding genuinely is far more effective than trying to guide the conversation through a preplanned pattern.

The FORM mnemonic mentioned in chapter 9 can likewise be a very helpful aid in finding things the two of you share in common. Just make sure it doesn't become rote or overdone. We've seen people cringe under the "So tell me, what do you like about where you live?"third-degree being hammered at them by well-intentioned but overly trained salespeople. If the other person feels like they're being interrogated, the opportunities for rapport dwindle rapidly.

One of the simplest techniques salespeople are taught is to use the other person's name, and use it often, as in, "You know, Jack, it's really great to meet you, Jack." As with many such techniques, this is a wonderful gesture of respect—and one that can easily go sour.

First, make sure you get the name *correct*. Going to the trouble of getting someone's name right is one of the simplest gestures of respect there is—and mispronouncing, mangling, or misremembering another's name is one of the surest ways to offend. We've heard people say, "Oh, I'm not good at names." This is like saying, "I'm not good at smiling." It's worth making the effort to *get* good at it.

And second, once you know you have someone's name right, then use it, but use it with respect, the way you would with a good friend. Calling someone by his or her name is like a verbal touch to the arm: done appropriately, it's a gesture of respect and intimacy. Overdone, it can feel invasive and creepy.

People are more sophisticated today than ever and are far more likely to sense it when a technique is being used on them. Skills and techniques can be a valuable part of your sales life, but they need to be kept in perspective. A good rule of thumb: when in doubt, be yourself.

And another rule of thumb: remember to keep your focus on *providing value for the other person*.

One of our readers, Laura, is a fund-raiser who works for a major metropolitan community service organization.

Every year, each person on our staff is given a fund-raising goal. The dollars we bring in go toward programs that keep our downtown vibrant, safe, clean, and well-managed.

This year I was given a $5,000 goal, but after reading *The Go-Giver*, I was able to bring in $15,000—about one-third of which I gave to other staff members to help them reach *their* goals.

How did she do this? Laura explains:

Every time I spoke to a downtown business owner or manager, I kept in mind that I was *giving value* to them—that in fact, I was willing to give *more* than I was requesting.

The "skill" that Laura employed was her focus on the fact that she was providing people with genuine value well beyond the dollar amount she was seeking—and she *tripled* her target.

Your compensation is an echo of your impact—and you will invariably have more impact on other people when you are focused on them, not on yourself.

The core skill involved in sales is *getting to know people*: engaging in relaxed conversation, listening to them closely, and letting yourself be guided by a genuine interest in them. Keep your focus on the other person—and your FORM will tend to take care of itself.

11. Curiosity

It occurred to Joe that up to this point, Pindar had never once asked him anything about his "homework" . . . so why was he asking now? A glance at Pindar told him the man wasn't checking up on him. He was asking because he genuinely wanted to know.

Salespeople have an expression: they talk about their "two-hundred-pound telephone." What they mean by this is that sometimes it feels really, really hard to pick up the phone and make that sales call.

Why? The greatest reluctance most salespeople have to making calls is that they find something about making those calls acutely uncomfortable. There is a host of reasons why this might occur, but they all boil down to the same thing: when you feel uncomfortable on a call, *you are thinking about yourself.*

We are sometimes taught that the way to step out of that discomfort is to whip up our own state of enthusiasm for our product or service. ("The last four letters of enthusiasm," goes the saying, "stand for I Am Sold Myself!") But enthusiasm doesn't necessarily promote *relatedness*. In fact, an over-the-top enthusiasm can put people off.

Besides, whipping up our own enthusiasm is, again, about me, me, me.

For all its considerable brilliance, the conscious human mind has some significant limitations. Your unconscious and autonomic nervous systems can process billions of data bits and run millions of physiological processes simultaneously—but your *conscious* mind has trouble remembering the ten digits of a phone number you heard thirty seconds ago. *And it cannot hold two different thoughts at the same time.*

This has profound implications for sales and selling. It means as long as you are thinking about you, you are not thinking about them. And that's not all. It also means that the most effective way to stop thinking about you is to think about them. And that is the secret to making your phone weightless: access your *genuine curiosity* about the person you're talking with.

Every one of us is innately curious. It's hardwired; it comes with being human. (If you don't believe it, spend fifteen minutes watching a baby, any baby.) But we don't all access that faculty with the same ease. It takes practice. At first, it may take consciously pushing yourself to be curious. It's well worth it. The single greatest skill in sales is a highly developed sense of interest in other people.

When you practice accessing your curiosity and genuine interest in others, *everyone* becomes fascinating. The bank teller, the coffee shop waitstaff, the lawn guy, the person at the airline ticket counter, even the telemarketer calling you at dinnertime to pitch you on *their* MacGuffin. You start to find that with your interest kindled, you can spark a conversation with virtually anyone, in virtually any situation. The truth about your "cold market" (that is, people you don't know) is that the moment you genuinely touch it, it begins to warm.

As the second law points out, the key to creating major income is touching as many lives as possible. This means getting to know a lot of people, and the only way you're really going to do that is if you are genuinely interested in them—not in the prospect of their buying your product or service, but in them, period.

If you're getting to know them in order to make a sale, you may find yourself running checklists in your mind and analyzing the conversation. "Have I asked them about where they live? What are they dissatisfied with in their lives? What are their hot buttons? Wait—what did they just say? I missed it!" On the other hand, if you're getting to know them because you're genuinely curious, you'll be far less likely to run your lists and practice your techniques.

Your attention is like a flashlight: it shines wherever you point it. The way you point it is with the silent questions you pose to yourself. If your questions are of this variety:

> How am I doing? Am I doing this right? Do they seem like a good customer for my product? Am I getting anywhere here? What should I say next?

. . . then you're pointing the flashlight of your attention on yourself. If your questions are more like this:

What's this person really like? What does she love to do most? What are some of her favorite moments? What's most important to her in all the world? Who *is* this person?

. . . then you're pointing the flashlight straight at them and evoking your own inborn sense of curiosity and empathy.

This is why it's essential that you put aside questions about money, "making the sale," success, your own survival, and anything else about *you*. If you focus on your curiosity and genuine interest in the other person, you won't have time to be nervous, self-conscious, manipulative, awkward, self-critical, or anything else.

You'll be too busy being interested in *them*.

12. Maturity

On their way into the building, someone pushed gruffly past them, complaining about how crowded it was, and bumped into Pindar. Much to Joe's surprise, Pindar simply smiled at him.

To be successful in sales, you have to learn to be in control of your emotions. This might seem at first like a contradiction; after all, the fourth law is called the Law of Authenticity. But there is nothing fake or inauthentic here. We're not talking about denying your feelings, but about keeping them in perspective and not letting them run your actions—about controlling them instead of letting them control you.

The ability to manage our own feelings so that they don't run us, what author Daniel Goleman calls *emotional intelligence*, is a critical characteristic in great salespeople. It boils down to one word: maturity.

We define emotional maturity as the ability to keep your focus on others' feelings even as you acknowledge and honor your own.

There will be circumstances—and yes, people—that may lead you to feel angry, frustrated, and exasperated. Note that wording: *lead* you to feel—not *make* you feel. No one can *make* another person feel angry, frustrated, resentful, or any other emotion. Other people say what they say and do what they do. What we say and do is up to us.

This is the difference between *responding* and *reacting*. when you react, you are letting external circumstances call the shots. When you respond, you are choosing your actions and feelings. Being mindful of this distinction allows us to live in life's solutions as opposed to its problems. And interestingly, it helps the other person to do the same: when you act with emotional maturity, it also tends to raise the emotional maturity level of all the conversations and exchanges in which you participate.

Developing a default mode of responding rather than reacting takes practice and isn't necessarily easy. However, it is a very profitable habit to gain. One effective way to do this is to envision a difficult situation and imagine yourself responding and handling it beautifully, and even to envision the other person's positive response. Like an astronaut going through flight simulations before an actual mission, you'll be much better equipped to handle similar situations when they happen.

The essence of professionalism, it has been said, is showing up for work even when you don't feel like it. Feelings and moods come and go. There may be times when you don't really feel like you're interested in this other person, don't feel like creating value for them, or don't even feel like being friendly. That's okay. Sometimes your foot falls asleep, but you haven't lost your foot—the feeling will come back. Take the action anyway.

But acting in a way you don't feel—isn't that being inauthentic? No, it is acting in a way you believe in. The truth is, actions often *precede* feelings. You'll be amazed how often, when you act in a caring way despite the fact that you don't feel especially caring at the moment, you will soon find yourself having those caring feelings after all.

As Gus says to Joe, "Sometimes you feel foolish, even look foolish, but you do the thing anyway."

Dixie Gillaspie, a very successful St. Louis business coach and consultant, shared this story with us; it's a wonderful example of how easy it can be to touch a life through the simple power of emotional maturity.

When I was young and naïve I had a little game I called, "What will it take to make you smile?" I smiled at everyone I met, and sometimes that was all it took. Sometimes it took a little conversation, sometimes it took more than one encounter. But I was out to prove I could make *anybody* smile.

In my early twenties I worked at an accounting office in Lawrence, Kansas. The partners all knew about my little game, and they told me they knew one client that I could never win against—he would *never* smile for me or anyone else. This client picked up his accounting every month but never came into the office; he just pulled up out front and honked, and we had to walk his reports out to his van. He never joked, he never chatted, and he never cracked a smile.

I said, "Wanna bet?"

For months Dixie walked out to the van, accounting reports in hand. And for months Dr. B. refused to smile. Dr. B. was a veterinarian who often had his dogs in the van with him, and Dixie thought he might warm up if she let him know how much she shared his love of animals. When he saw that his dogs took a liking to her, he thawed a little—but he did not smile.

From July to November I played my game, losing to his straight face every month but never giving up.

Then came December.

For an accounting firm, December is the brink of craziness. Between month-end accounting, year-end accounting, and gearing up for the impending tax season, holiday parties are an afterthought at best. I hadn't even noticed that Dr. B.'s accounting was sitting on the shelf, waiting for me to take it out—and I certainly was not prepared for what I saw when I looked up from my desk: there was Dr. B., standing in the doorway of our office, leaning heavily on a cane with one hand and holding, what was that in the other? A holiday tin?!

Dr. B. limped slowly to my desk and held out the tin. He said he wanted me to know how much my unflagging cheerfulness had meant to him, especially that last summer when his gout was the worst and he hurt all the time and was embarrassed to try to walk because it was so hard. He said the chocolates weren't much, but he hoped I had a Merry Christmas. He put the tin in my hands.

And he *smiled*.

III. The Law
of Influence

*Your influence is determined by
how abundantly you place
other people's interests first.*

13. Build Networks

Have you ever wondered what makes people attractive? I mean,
genuinely attractive? Magnetic? . . . They love to give. That's why
they're attractive. Givers attract.   —PINDAR

It's fairly straightforward to see the impact you're having on people you meet. The secret to developing a vast and thriving sales business is the impact you have on people you have *not* yet met—people whose lives you touch, at least in some measure, before you ever lay eyes on them or have a conversation with them.

What could possibly cause your impact to reach out beyond the people you know to touch the lives of those you have never even met? Your influence. The strength and reach of your influence determines how many of those people you'll reach and the quality of that reach. The third law raises the effect of the second law to a higher order of magnitude, multiplying your personal *impact* through the spreading medium of your *influence*.

The nature of genuine influence is often misunderstood.

We often think of influence as the ability to get other people to do what we want them to. But genuine influence accrues to those who become known as the sort of person who is committed to helping other people get what *they* want.

Genuine influence flows from *reputation*. When you set out to create a career in sales, your single most important task is the building of reputation. Financial capital, savings, company position or rank in an organization, business assets—all these can be gained and lost and gained again. All are inconsequential in comparison to reputation, which is a house that, once burned down, is very difficult to rebuild.

When Archimedes, the brilliant architect of ancient Greece, discovered the principle of leverage, he declared, "Give me a place to stand, and I can move the world." You have that place to stand: your reputation.

In *The 8th Habit*, Stephen R. Covey distinguishes between influence by title or position, which he calls *formal authority*, and genuine influence, which he calls *moral authority*. Gandhi never held any formal position, Covey points out, yet because of his tremendous moral authority he became the father of what is today the largest democracy in the world. George Washington had such moral authority that it was virtually a foregone conclusion that he would lead his fragile new nation as its first president. Washington's election to the presidency did not *create* his influence, it was the natural *result* of his influence.

The distinction between structural and moral authority is like the difference between pushing and pulling. How far can you push a column of air into a room with an ordinary window fan? Not far: within a few feet it starts doubling back on itself. But reverse the fan's position so that it is blowing out, and you can *pull* that same column of air from a single open window clear on the other side of the house, even hundreds of feet away.

Or think of it this way: how far can you push a rope?

In sales, *pushing* is telling people what you want; *pulling* is finding out what *they* want. If I enter a conversation just itching to give my "elevator pitch" and tell you all about this fantastic, premium, top-of-the-line MacGuffin I represent, it's all push, no matter how much I might pretty it up with qualifying questions and chitchat about your family.

Pushing on people doesn't move them any farther than it does air or a rope. But ask them about themselves, find out what *their* interests are, put *their* interests ahead of your own, and you can "pull" people from vast distances. The influence created by pushing does not carry far. The influence created through pulling is limitless.

Which brings us to networking.

Too often what people call networking is really a disguised version of tit for tat, a type of interpersonal accounting system that measures favors given against favors sought. To be sure, a dog-*help*-dog world is a kinder and gentler environment for doing business than a dog-*eat*-dog world. But it's still a billiard-ball variety of arithmetic scorekeeping, where the focus rests heavily on the implied question, "What have you done for me lately?"

The Law of Influence turns this mode on its head, approaching each business relationship with the question, "What have I done for *you* lately?"

Bea Salabi is someone who goes all out when she gives; it's just her nature. She serves on the board of directors for the local Habitat for Humanity, sponsors a family of eight children, and goes out of her way to help anyone and everyone she can. (One summer, she took fifteen hundred local underprivileged children to the movies—and gave them all popcorn.)

One day a couple Bea knew from church told her about a local woman who was having her house foreclosed on. They said they wanted to buy the house to prevent the foreclosure. They would hang onto the home, they told Bea, until the woman was able to buy it back from them. Bea was running a mortgage company at the time; could her company help them arrange the mortgage? Bea not only agreed, she set up their mortgage for free, refusing to take a single cent from the transaction.

The couple was so impressed with Bea that they started spreading the word about her. The torrent of referrals Bea got resulted in more than *two dozen* closed transactions—every one of which did indeed earn substantial commissions for Bea.

Great salespeople grow great networks because they focus their actions on looking out for *the other person's* interests and serving *their* needs. They prefer to give the credit away than to seek it for themselves. Rather than aspire to be kings, they seek to be kingmakers. They are constantly on the lookout for ways they can help to elevate other people's lives—and in the process they become enormously influential themselves.

14. Fuzzy Influence

[Sam] looked directly at Joe. "Do you know what I mean by 'network'?"

In fact, Joe had just been thinking that networking was something he indeed knew all about, but the question caught him by surprise and he quickly shook his head. "No—I mean, yes, I think I do." He paused. "But I'll bet I don't," he finished lamely.

What Joe did not yet grasp was what Sam and Pindar called the Golden Rule of Business: *All things being equal, people will do business with and refer business to those people they know, like, and trust.*

Where do great customers come from? From the gravitational pull of our influence, which is our capacity to engender those *know, like, and trust* feelings in others.

The Internet has given us a powerful way of extending our reach to thousands of people we wouldn't have known otherwise, at virtually no cost. Incredible. But what's more incredible is that *this has always been the case*. Even without computers, every single individual is the hub of his or her own sphere of influence—and that sphere's potential is immense.

The great automobile salesman Joe Girard, hailed by *The Guinness Book of World Records* as the greatest salesperson in the world, coined the "Law of 250," which says that on average, every person has about 250 people in his life who would show up at his wedding or funeral. Joe concluded that if he treated one customer poorly, he had lost not one sale but a potential 250 sales. On the other hand, he reasoned, if he treated that same person well, he had just had a positive influence on 250 people, and not just on one.

Each individual has a sphere of influence that encompasses an average of 250 people—each of whom has his or her *own* sphere of influence encompassing 250 more people each, and so on. *Every human being is the center of his or her own human Internet.*

Which means that every single time you meet one new person and cultivate a relationship with that person to the point where they know, like, and trust you, you have just increased your own personal sphere of influence not by one but by a potential 250 at least, and likely a great many more. And just as you are positioned at the center of your own network, so are they each positioned at the center of theirs.

Who are all these thousands of people? They are people whom you've never met or perhaps even heard of—so far. And yet through the strength of your influence, they may well hear about *you*.

We've all heard the expression, "It's not what you know, it's *who* you know." But that doesn't quite describe it accurately. It's not who you know, it's who knows *you* and who knows *about* you, even if they haven't actually met you.

Sean Woodruff, who owns a company that manufactures

and sells trailer hitches for RVs, recently told us about a customer who was having a good deal of difficulty understanding and installing Sean's product. Sean gave the man his cell phone number—and over the next twenty-four hours, the man called him for help *eighteen times*. When the man finally got all squared away, he told Sean he was deeply grateful for Sean's patience.

He called today to thank me and tell me how much he loves the product. "For the past week," he said, "I've been driving around the country in my RV telling everyone about how patient you were with me!"

Two hours later, I received a call from another person telling me he had been considering a competitor of mine, but after talking to this customer, he had decided to let go of the competitor and order my product. He told me how blessed he felt that he had crossed paths with this customer of mine.

He felt blessed? So did I!

So where will your best customers come from? The classic view is that there are two places to look: your *warm market* and *cold market*, that is, people you know and those you don't. But the chances are good that the majority of your best customers will come from neither of those places but from the fuzzy area in between the two—that neither hot nor cold domain that you might call your *fuzzy market*.

Your fuzzy market includes all those people you *vaguely* know: not exactly friends, but not exactly strangers, either. The teller at your bank, your kids' friends' moms, a distant college classmate from years ago. People whose faces you know, if not their names. And it also includes people who know the people you know: friends of friends of friends.

There is some interesting and rather famous science behind this. In 1970, Harvard sociologist Mark Granovetter studied several hundred professional, technical, and managerial workers in Newton, Massachusetts, to see how they had found their current jobs. More than half had learned about their positions through personal contacts. This was no big surprise—but the next part was: of those who had used a personal contact to find a job, only 16 percent saw that contact "often" (that is, the contact was a close friend), and more than 55 percent saw that contact only "occasionally."

According to Dr. Granovetter, you are not very likely to learn about a new opportunity through someone you know well, because your friends occupy the same world you do. You are far more likely to learn about something new from someone you know *vaguely*. Those with whom we share what Dr. Granovetter calls "weak ties" have more influence on us than either strangers or our close friends.* You never know *where* your greatest customers will come from—and it will probably be from where you do not expect.

On the very first page of *The Go-Giver*, Joe learns about a competitor he's never heard of before, someone who has seemingly appeared in Joe's life to make him miserable by stealing away a key client. Yet by the last chapter, the two men have become good friends and business partners.

*Granovetter, Mark. "The Strength of Weak Ties," *American Journal of Sociology*, Vol. 78, Issue 6, May 1973, pp. 1360-1380.

Pure fiction? Not really; it happens all the time. One reader wrote us with this story about a good friend of hers, Dave:

Dave worked in a family-owned foundry business in New Jersey. One year when the family went on vacation, the night watchman left a kerosene lamp lit; the lamp caught fire and the entire production area burned to the ground. Dave's family was out of business.

While they set about the tedious task of rebuilding the place, Dave called on other foundries—ostensibly his competitors—to see if he could job out his foundry's workload to them, hoping to ensure that all his customers would be taken care of. At one foundry a man named Chris befriended Dave and agreed not only to handle his customers' orders but to give them priority. Chris got nothing special in return; he just wanted to help Dave out. Because of him, Dave's foundry was able to stay in business while it was being rebuilt.

Several years passed; then one day Chris called to tell Dave that he had lost his job. Although he asked for no special favors, Dave put Chris and his family on his foundry's health care rolls and kept them there—until one day, when Dave received another phone call from Chris.

"Dave," said Chris, "I have a new job. In fact, I've just been appointed officer of this company I'm going to work for. You are my first phone call. We have some business to do together, my friend." He proceeded to send *all* the new company's work to Dave's foundry, which turned out to be a fortune's worth of business.

"Appearances can be deceiving," Pindar tells Joe in *The Go-Giver*. "Truth is, they nearly always are." Success most often comes from the unlikeliest of places. How do you find your greatest customers? You don't. *They find you*.

Exactly when, and from exactly where? Hard to say: those details will always be a little fuzzy.

Exactly how? They are drawn by your influence.

15. The Perfect "Pitch"

I never actually tried to get Pindar's help on this deal. I never even brought his name up to Carl Kellerman. I suppose I screwed up big time—but if I had to do it over, I think I'd do the same thing. You know?
                                                                    —JOE

The part of selling that most aspiring salespeople have the hardest time with is prospecting. This is simply because we're all *people*, and most of us want to be liked by other people. Knocking on doors and making sales calls doesn't seem like a great way to do that. People don't *like* being prospected, and we all know it. It's no wonder we dread the prospect of prospecting.

If you're going to be great at selling, you need to find a way to go about it that feels a lot more comfortable, both for you and for the other person. And that comes down to the question of *the pitch*.

In just a moment, we're going to let you in on a sales secret that is worth a fortune. This is the secret of how to make the perfect sales pitch, first time and every time—

and best of all, this secret is contained *in a single word*. But first, let's set the scene.

You're at a chamber of commerce mixer, Rotary Club or Business and Professional Women meeting, a social party, a charity event, or PTA meeting—any gathering of the sort of people you might like to have as your customers.

"Wait—the PTA? Aren't people going to think I'm obnoxious and out of line prospecting at an event like that?"

Yes they will, if you do it the way salespeople often do, which is to cruise the event like a pickup artist wannabe at a singles bar. The key is to go in not with the goal of "hitting on" people, but with the goal of meeting people and making a few new friends. Not making new friends-so-you-can-cleverly-turn-them-into-prospects. Just making friends. Why? To make friends.

You've met someone, and you're in a conversation. You feel you've got some pretty good rapport going. Now what?

Most of us have been taught that in this situation, we're supposed to look for the earliest opportunity to tell people about what we do—or to create that opportunity with a clever "turn question." You ask the person what *they* do in order to subtly maneuver them into asking you what *you* do, and then you launch your cleverly scripted *elevator pitch*:

"Well, I'm in the health and wealth business."

But wait: let's back up a moment. Our goal is to create value for this person, right? A pitch is not something you do *for* someone; it's something you do *to* someone. And think about baseball: what's the purpose of a pitch? To strike the other person out. Where's the value?

If you walk into the party, wind up that throwing arm, and fire off your best fastball, all you'll probably accomplish is to push the other person into thinking, "Oh boy, here's another salesperson who has some bridge he wants to sell me." At the best, they get kind of glassy-eyed, feign politeness, and look for a discreet opportunity to back away. At worst, you've annoyed them—and added one more bit of evidence to the pile in that ongoing case in the court of world opinion, The People v. Obnoxious Salespeople.

"Okay, so I'm having this wonderful conversation. How do I turn that into connecting them to my MacGuffin without coming off as obnoxious or manipulative?"

Here's how: you don't even mention your MacGuffin. You don't talk about it *at all*.

When you first meet this person, there are three words you need to remember when it comes to your business: *they don't care*. Sure, *you're* excited about your product or service. Sure, *you* can see how much they need it, how much it will enhance or even change their life, how much value it would create for them if *you* could just tell them about it. But this isn't about you: it's about them.

Now we're ready for that one-word secret to making the perfect sales pitch:

Don't.

The secret to the perfect sales pitch is *to have no pitch*.

Early in Bob's career as a speaker, there was one major corporate client with whom he really wanted to do business, but try though he might, he couldn't seem to get his foot in the door. "This was my Big Kahuna," says Bob, "but I couldn't even *find* that door, let alone figure out how to stick my foot in it."

At a speakers' convention, Bob met a successful speaker named Greg, who was there with his family, and they struck up a friendship. Bob kept bumping into them at events, and as their friendship grew, Bob started looking for ways to add value to Greg's life.

One day a client called to engage me for a talk, but I was already booked for that date, so I suggested the client contact Greg instead. Before long the same thing happened a second time, and then a third. Another time I was talking with an editor at a magazine who had published my articles, and I referred him to Greg as a possible writer for their magazines.

A few years after they met, Bob learned something astonishing about Greg: one of his clients was none other than the Big Kahuna!

I knew I could probably come right out and ask for Greg's help—but it just didn't feel right. I didn't want him to feel that, because I had gone out of my way to help him, that he "owed" me something. So I never did ask for his help.

I did ask for his advice, though: did he have any idea who might be the best person for me to contact there?

"Tell you what," said Greg. "I'll have my contact get in touch with *you*." And sure enough, the very

next day my phone rang. The Big Kahuna was calling *me*.

And although Bob never "pitched" them, they did indeed become a client of his—a client who in the years
since has generated several million dollars in sales for his
business.

Some salespeople have been taught what is called the
"three-foot rule," which says that everyone who comes
within three feet is fair game to pitch to about your product. But what if this person doesn't *want* to hear about your
product? Doesn't she have a choice?

Your first priority in any encounter should be to add
value to the other person's life, that is, to enrich or enhance
their life in some way. Or at the very least, not to *subtract*
value, which means not to irritate them, suck energy from
them, intimidate them, bully them, pressure them, or ma-
nipulate them.

Great salespeople live by the same code as the physi-
cian's Hippocratic oath: *first, do no harm*. It's something
like the goal of conscious agriculture: leave the soil in better shape than you found it. Future generations will want
to farm this soil, too.

Part of maturity in sales is coming to grips with the re-
alization that not everyone is a prospective customer, no
matter how close to you they may be in feet *or* in common
interests. Not everyone wants to buy your MacGuffin—in
fact, not everyone wants to *hear* about your MacGuffin.

Great salespeople turn the three-foot rule on its head by
making it about the other person. The Go-Giver salesperson's three-foot rule goes something like this:

Anyone within three feet is worth getting to know better.

That said, when you're at an event with a lot of people, don't feel you need to meet everyone. Your aim is to have fun and make friends. Go for quality, not quantity. And *don't pitch*.

"But if I don't pitch, then what *do* I do?"

Great question. And that's exactly what you do: *ask great questions*—which is what we'll look at next.

16. Great Questions

Go looking for the best in people, and you'll be amazed at how much talent, ingenuity, empathy, and good will you'll find. —PINDAR

The traditional sales process centers on the presentation. The Go-Giver sales process focuses on the *connection*, which happens more through listening than through talking. And the best way to listen productively is to ask great questions. To become great at sales, learning how to ask great questions is in many ways more important than learning how to make a great presentation. Let's look at a few great questions.

How did you get started in the [fill in the blank] business?

Clever? Not especially. Mundane? Absolutely—and people *love* to answer this question. We sometimes call it the "movie-of-the-week" question because it invites others to tell the story of their life. It is also a question they have rarely if ever had the chance to answer, because most people don't care enough to ask this question. But you do.

Here's another:

What do you enjoy most about what you do?

Asking this question flies in the face of most traditional sales teaching, which says you should reach right in to the prospect's heart and tear it out, showing them how inadequate their world is without you and your terrific product or service. "What do you *hate* most about what you do?" we are taught to ask—and might as well add, "and while we're at it, how about this wretched excuse for a life you're living?"

The idea of this conventional approach is that it helps you establish need. But establishing need is not what we're after here: we're after *creating value*. Asking this "What do you enjoy most . . . ?" question evokes pleasure, appreciation, and pride in the other person. Your conversation serves to remind them of the best things in their life. And they'll remember that.

In fact, that is exactly what makes these *great* questions, and the reason Bob calls them Feel-Good Questions: they lead the other person into a conversation that *makes them feel good*.

Here are a few more great Feel-Good Questions:

What do you see as most unique or special about your company or your business?

What advice would you give someone just starting out in the [fill in the blank] business?

What's the strangest or funniest thing you've seen happen in your business?

What significant changes have you seen in your profession in, say, the past ten years?

What do you see as the coming trends in the [fill in the blank] business?

To truly experience the power of these questions, take a moment to go through them yourself, one by one, imagining that someone is asking them of you. As you answer, be aware of how you feel. You'll begin to get a tangible sense of the kind of value a great question can create for another person. It can allow them to offer their expert opinion, brag a bit about their strengths, muse on those aspects of their business that intrigue them, please them, fascinate them, and gratify them most. It turns the flashlight of their attention on what's *great* about their life.

There is nothing slick or clever about these questions, no special wording you have to get just right. At their essence, they come from your being genuinely curious about the person's life. And by the way, you will likely never ask them *all* in one conversation. Often two or three will do fine.

At some point, when you sense the rapport between you is strong, you may like to ask what Bob calls the One Key Question:

Jack, how can I know if someone I'm talking to is a good prospect for you?

Depending on what that person does, the most apt phrase might be "good customer," "good contact," "good connection," or simply "someone you'd like to meet."

Again, this invites them to tell you all about *them*. It also communicates the feeling that you are genuinely interested in adding value to their life. And before they can be open to your opportunity or products, they first have to be open to you.

There's no hidden, tricky "turn" that gets them talking about you and your business. No trapdoors, no hinged panels, no smoke and mirrors. This is not a sneaky "technique," it's actually just what it looks like: authentic conversation.

Bob once learned from a CEO he'd just met that the man's daughter Beth had just graduated college. "Tell me," Bob said about five minutes into the conversation, "how can I know if someone I'm speaking with would be a good connection for Beth as she starts her career?" The CEO was intrigued with the question, and after a few moments' thought, he answered it carefully.

A few weeks later, Bob introduced the man to someone who did indeed turn out to be a good connection for Beth. In fact, he eventually brought her on as an intern, helping her launch a successful career. Do you suppose Bob eventually got the CEO's business? He did—and quite a few high quality referrals as well.

Sometimes it happens that the first time you strike up a conversation with someone, that person wants or needs to know about your MacGuffin right then and there, and you find yourself setting an appointment or getting down to brass tacks. But don't count on that happening too often.

On the other end of the spectrum, there will be times

when you meet someone new, and the pleasant conversation you have ends up being a pleasant conversation and nothing more. All you have done is added a tiny bit more substance to our overall experience of value on planet earth. Not a bad day's work.

Here is something that can be very useful to remember. In order for your sales business to thrive, *someone* needs to say yes to your MacGuffin. But it doesn't need to be *this* person. So relax, enjoy the conversation—and walk out of there with a new friend.

17. Follow-Through

Forget about fifty-fifty, son. Fifty-fifty's a losing proposition. The only winning proposition is one hundred percent. *Make your win about the other person. Forget win-win*—focus on the other person's win.
—SAM ROSEN

The most important questions prospects ask are the very ones most salespeople miss—because people never ask them out loud. They may not even be thinking them consciously themselves. But they're asking them, all right, and the answers will make or break their trust in you. These questions include:

Can I trust you?

Will you do what you said you'd do?

Do I really matter to you?

You cannot effectively answer these unspoken questions in English, Spanish, Japanese, or Urdu. There is only one language in which you can answer them: *action*. This is why follow-through is everything, not just in your golf swing, but also in friendships, in marriages, in business— and especially in sales.

Sales trainings usually use the term follow-*up*, which means continuing or repeating something that has already been done. We like the term follow-*through* even better, since it means completing a process or action and taking it to its fullest conclusion.

The essence of follow-through is this: in the hours, days, and weeks after meeting and talking with your new acquaintance, continue looking for ways to add value to their life. For example, you can send a personalized, handwritten thank-you note that says what a pleasure it was to meet them. It's such a simple thing, and it speaks volumes.

One of the greatest ways of creating value for people is by connecting them to other people and suggesting ways they can do business with each other or benefit in some other way from the relationship. In this way, you serve as a catalyst for others' greatness. The cost? Nothing. The value? Incalculable.

You might also send them information they may find interesting or valuable—not about your product or service but about something they're personally interested in. If Anne collects antique music boxes or Jack's daughter is a star high school soccer player and you send along some information you found about antique music boxes or high school soccer, you're adding value.

Sometimes you'll come across a book or CD that seems perfect for this person, and you might buy a copy and send it to them. Do this judiciously, though, because spending anything more than a few dollars can make the recipient feel a little awkward, like they now owe you something. Sometimes creating that extra value is as simple as sending a link to an article you've read online that might benefit them. And even here you have to use your judgment, so that you don't cross the line from helpful to annoying. Follow through with a strong heart and a light touch.

When the occasion presents itself (and because you are constantly on the lookout for such occasions, it often will), you can even refer new business to your acquaintance. Now *that's* adding value.

All these gestures serve the same end and convey the same message: that you have put their interests first. They all answer those unspoken questions with a firm *yes*: *yes*, they can trust you; *yes*, you are someone who does what you say you'll do; *yes*, they genuinely matter to you.

It's easy to get overwhelmed these days with the proliferation of communication avenues on the Internet. We're not advocating you get wrapped up in every social networking site that comes along. Life is too precious to waste time chasing your tail and gazing at web site after web site. But do whatever it takes to get organized with your email and correspondence and invest the time in staying in touch. It's well worth the investment.

Gary Vaynerchuk, the founder of WineLibraryTV.com, was managing his dad's liquor store in New Jersey when he had the idea of creating a web-based wine-tasting show. Today his show draws audiences of nearly one hundred thousand people per day—a brilliant application of the first and second laws.

A man of boundless energy who is incredibly generous

with his time, Gary is also a master of the Law of Influence. He receives hundreds of emails every day—and takes the time to answer each and every one of them personally. And that's one of the secrets to his remarkable success: his fans know he cares about them.

People sometimes teach sales by comparing it to fishing. Thus, you catch them with a "hook," and sometimes you have to "lay out a lot of lines" and wait patiently before you can "reel in a big one." This is also why salespeople often talk about "landing" a client.

Nothing against fishing, but we think the sales process is a lot more like farming. You prepare the soil; you plant seeds; you water, weed, nurture, and cultivate. In other words, *follow through*. Not every seed takes root; it may be only one seed in ten, or one in twenty.

Which connections will bear fruit, and when? It depends; different relationships and situations take different amounts of time. Just as with the farmer's partnership with the soil, sun, and seasons, the exact timing is *not up to you*. What *is* up to you is the quality of your follow-through.

But know this: if you prepare the soil well and are careful in your cultivation, you will reap a harvest—silos full.

18. Your Serve

If you notice, what I said was, "Share her coffee." What you said was, "Make a killing." Do you see the difference? —PINDAR

Somewhere along in this process, it will come time to explain what you do. This may happen the very first time you and the other person meet, or it may happen only weeks or months into the process.

"Wait a minute!" you might be thinking. "It might happen the first time we meet? But didn't you say I should keep the focus of our conversation on *them*?"

Yes, to the extent that it feels natural to do so. But that doesn't mean you should be evasive. If they ask what it is you do, the natural thing to do is *tell* them. Sooner or later, whether it's because they themselves might be interested in looking at your product, or they know someone who might be, or they simply want to understand what it is you do, there comes a point when it's time to let the MacGuffin out of the bag.

What do you say?

Traditional sales training often teaches that this is the moment you've been waiting for, the moment when you get to launch your "elevator pitch." Imagine you are in an elevator, so the thinking goes, and someone walks in: *quick*, you have thirty seconds to explain to them what you do before the doors open again and they walk out of your life forever!

But great salespeople don't pitch. We're not going for a strikeout. What we're doing here is having a natural, genuine conversation.

Let's shift the image for a moment from baseball to a friendly game of tennis. Go-Givers don't pitch—but they do *serve*. If the purpose of a pitch is to strike the other guy out, the purpose of a serve is to hit the ball over the net so the other guy can hit it back, and you two can enjoy the game together. (It is, after all, a *friendly* game of tennis.) In other words, you want to explain what it is you do, clearly and succinctly, in such a way that the other person gets *engaged in the game*.

How do you do that? It has to do with the difference between *features* and *benefits*. You've probably been taught about this. Most of us have—and yet, oddly, many of us still talk features. Perhaps it's because the terms and definitions are a little abstract. Let's make this crystal clear:

A *feature* is about your MacGuffin.

A *benefit* is about the other person.

People are not looking for features, or what something *is*; they are looking for benefits, or what it can *do for them*. The most helpful answer to the question "So, what do *you* do?" is one that explains what you have to offer in such a way that the other person immediately grasps the benefits of what your product or service will do for them (or for others they know).

A pitch is *me*-focused. A serve is *them*-focused.

Your serve is your brief answer to the question "What do you do?" that describes *the benefits people derive from doing business with you*.

This is worth investing some time to explore. Take a piece of paper and brainstorm the benefits of your business and the product or service you sell. As you do this, you'll get the best results if, instead of asking the question, "What is it I'm selling?" you ask the question, "Why would people want to buy from me—what benefits would that give them?" This shifts your focus from you and your MacGuffin to the other person and *their* interests.

Features are answers to the question "What?"

Benefits are answers to the question "Why?"

You can tell when a conversation goes beyond the more superficial, just-getting-to-know-you stage and starts becoming more genuinely personal when it moves from *what* to *why*.

A *what* conversation is about questions such as what's your name, what do you do for a living, where do you live, what's your family like, what's your neighborhood like, what school did you go to, and so forth.

A *why* conversation starts going deeper and exploring the person's values. Why do you do what you do? Why do you live here in this area? *Why* conversations drive to the question of what genuinely matters. *Why* conversations are where real connections are made.

Back to your conversation. When your new friend asks you what you do, the best way to serve the ball in such a way that they can easily get engaged and hit it back to you is to give an answer that is *pure benefits*.

Listen to these answers, and to how they land when you lob them over the net.

I'm in the insurance business. *(Thud.)*

I sell leading-edge, top-of-the-line skin care products. *(Thud.)*

I'm in real estate. *(Thud.)*

You see how that happens? They are statements that go nowhere, because they really don't invite any reply. Instead, you want to serve a ball that the other person can lob back: a statement that answers their question in an interesting way and tends to encourage an engaged response. For example:

I help people protect their families and plan for a healthy financial future.

I build people's health and confidence through anti-aging technology.

I help people successfully sell their homes and own their dream home.

These refer to the same three businesses as above, only described in terms of their benefits, that is to say, not "what I do" but "what I help others do."

Here is the litmus test: when you say it, does the other person say, "Oh," or "*Oh?*" A statement of features tends to land with a thud; you can hear it in the person's voice: "Uh-huh. Oh, interesting. Yeah, I know someone who's in that." A serve of benefits tends to draw the other person forward with interest and usually some sort of question in response. "Really! How do you do *that*?"

You served; they hit it back; the ball is in play.

Here are a few more examples of *serves*. Note how each focuses on the benefits, not the features:

STOCKBROKER: I help people create and manage wealth.

SUPPLEMENTAL HEALTH INSURANCE REP: We help companies protect their employees from financial disaster—at absolutely no cost to the employer.

LONG-TERM CARE INSURANCE REP: We help people protect their hard-earned assets from one of life's greatest financial catastrophes.

CHIROPRACTOR: I help people heal themselves naturally, without medication.

LITIGATING ATTORNEY: My firm helps people resolve disputes and avoid needless costly consequences.

Will they always hit the ball back perfectly? No, and it doesn't matter. And that brings us to one last—and most crucial of all—aspect of your serve: you don't have to "get it right."

There is an expression in sales: *You can't say the wrong thing to the right person, and you can't say the right thing to the wrong person.*

Whether or not this person is interested in your MacGuffin is ultimately up to them, not you. If you think you have to get this exactly right in order to make your business a success, then this is a perfect time to take the pressure off.

Remember that you cannot *make a sale*. Only *they* can do that. What you can do is *create value*.

It's your serve.

19. Posture

"Being broke and being rich are both decisions. You make them up, right up here." [Nicole] tapped her finger to her temple. *"Everything else is just how it plays out."*

If people want to do business with those they know, like, and trust, they generally do *not* want to do business with those who appear to *need* them too much. If being pushy and aggressive repels people (and it does), then so does being overly eager and needy.

The problem here is that you may in fact be needy. After all, if you're counting on sales to earn the income to support yourself and your family, then your need is genuine. This can devolve into a vicious circle: the more strongly you need the income, the more needy you feel, the more you project that feeling, the more others pick up on it and feel like backing away, the harder it is to earn the income you need, the more urgently you need it, and so on.

This is where emotional clarity and discipline come into play.

Emotional *clarity* is your understanding that there is a difference between your economic need (which is real) and your emotional need for this person to be the solution to that economic need. Emotional *discipline* is your ability to hold onto that clarity and consistently choose your responses to each situation, rather than reacting impulsively.

There is a word for this combination of clarity and discipline: *posture*.

By posture we don't mean acting phony, pretending to be someone you're not, or "fake it till you make it." Quite the contrary. By posture we mean shaking off doubts and insecurities and stepping into the truth of who you are and the value of what you have to offer, without emotional attachment to any specific outcome.

This is something like when your mother used to say, "Stand up straight!" She didn't mean "Stand up as if you were someone else," she meant, "Stand up as yourself!"

Part of posture is staying clear on what you cannot control. This turns out to be quite an impressive list: you cannot control the weather, the state of the economy, the score of your favorite sports team—or what the person you're talking with is going to do next. Whether this other person buys your product or is even interested in your product is entirely up to them. You cannot control the outcome.

What you *can* control are the actions you take, the words you speak, and especially the thoughts you hold. Why "especially" your thoughts? Because your thoughts often communicate just as loudly as your words and deeds—and sometimes even more so.

It's helpful here to remember that the conscious mind can hold only one thought at a time. The only way you can succumb to the sense of feeling needy is when your focus is on yourself. So let's ask ourselves a different question. The question before you is not whether *you* need this person to be interested in your MacGuffin; the question is, do *they* need your MacGuffin?

It's not about you: it's about them.

To be successful, you need some people to show interest in what you're offering and, ultimately, to buy it. But the world is a big place and your "funnel" is vast. Because you've been putting the first three Laws of Stratospheric Success into practice, your reputation is growing and your influence is spreading: people you've never met or even heard of are hearing about *you*, right at this very minute. Your business will touch the lives of many, many people— but you don't need *this particular person* to be one of them.

At the same time, you also believe in your MacGuffin 100 percent and know full well the wonderful benefits this particular person stands to gain from taking a look at your product or service. Your success does not depend on this person saying yes—but their getting the full benefits of what you have to offer *does*. So, breathe, relax, and give this conversation your very best. There's not a lot riding on the outcome for *you*—but there could be for *them*.

Actress-producer-writer Sybil Temtchine recalls that when she first began working in the entertainment industry, she could not have felt more authentic. "I simply didn't know any different," says Sybil. But over the following few years, she began losing touch with that authenticity.

Out of fear that the initial success I'd had might all go away, that maybe I wasn't *enough*, I started to conform—and slowly but surely all the good things in my life started going away.

When you are trying to do something, like Joe in *The Go-Giver* trying to make his third-quarter numbers, you can become someone you are not: someone who forgets how to experience and give joy through the process, someone who lives out of fear.

When an unexpected personal crisis knocked her briefly out of work, Sybil took stock of her life and reexamined what was truly important to her.

Sometimes it's when it all goes away that we find out what we're made of. I found out that in our own ways, we are *all* good enough.

Resuming her career, Sybil went on to even greater success—on her own terms.

Having developed a concept for a film about women and self-esteem, Sybil decided to raise the money for production herself. She went to a local bookstore to search out every woman author she could find whose writing touched on the topic of empowering women, from Suze Orman to Marianne Williamson. She wrote to every one of the two hundred authors on her list—and three out of four wrote back. Some sent checks; others offered introductions and referrals. Before long Sybil had raised half her budget and preproduction for her film *Audrey* was under way.

Still, as satisfying as that was, says Sybil, the external accomplishment was not the greatest measure of fulfillment.

Believing in yourself is the true success—because nothing can take that away.

What was it that enabled Sybil to contact world-famous authors out of the blue and successfully raise hundreds of thousands of dollars for her project? She knew who she was. She had *posture*.

20. The Competition

[Joe] clicked off the phone, set it on his desk, and stared at it, lost in disbelief at what he'd just done. "This guy just blows me off—and I give him a referral?" he muttered. "And throw some good business at a competitor?!"

The chances are excellent that once you're in a conversation about your particular field, at some point you'll be confronted with the perfect opportunity to bash the competition. This is a character-revealing moment. In a few sentences, a few words—even a gesture or a look—you can cause the relationship to grow suddenly deeper and stronger, or deal it a fatal blow.

We are big believers in competition, but it's important to remember why it exists and what it's doing there. We live in a society that permits and encourages competition because of the value it contributes to the health of the whole. This is not some abstract economic theory. Good competition keeps you on your toes, raising the bar for what a business like yours can do. Good competition pushes and stretches the limits of what's possible.

In a very real sense, your competition is your best friend.

But sometimes people get confused about this and think the correct goal is to destroy your competition. What a tragic error. If you could succeed in destroying all your competitors, you would be raining down destruction on your own field.

Happily, salespeople are often taught never to speak ill of their competition, and that doing so will only make *them* look bad. Unfortunately, most salespeople have been taught not to say anything *good* about their competition, either.

Whenever you're speaking to a prospect and they bring up your competitor, go out of your way to say something nice about him or her. Because you're a nice person? No. (Although we're sure you are indeed a very nice person). Because when you compliment your competitor, you are also demonstrating respect—and *respect earns respect*.

If in a conversation you tear down your competitor, it actually diminishes you in the other person's eyes. On the other hand, when you take care to say something positive about your competition, it actually builds you up in their eyes. These are the messages that register for the other person, consciously or not:

You are confident. Knocking the competition is one way people often try to *act* confident. Ironically, it telegraphs precisely the opposite message. But if you not only refrain from speaking ill of your competitors but actually speak highly of them, then you must be *genuinely* confident. And confidence breeds confidence.

You are successful. If you are genuinely confident, then it stands to reason you must also be successful. After all, unsuccessful people don't have that sort of genuine confidence in themselves.

You are safe. If you speak that highly of your competition, then this person knows they'll never have to worry about what you say about *them* behind their back.

John tells a story about shopping for a car that shows how that difference in attitude—bashing versus respect, bravado versus genuine confidence—cost one dealer tens of thousands of dollars and *earned* it for another. He set out to visit three different import dealers with the goal of comparing both their cars *and* the experiences he had in each place. Here's what happened:

First was the local BMW man, Mike.

I'd been there a few times, checking out a few cars on the floor, and Mike remembered me vaguely. He took my kids and me for a test spin, and on our drive we made small talk. I left the lot sort of liking Mike, but feeling I hadn't learned much about the car or gotten much value.

Next was Lexus.

The nearest Lexus dealer was a good ninety minutes away, and I was too busy to go that distance. No problem. Tink Doyle from Lexus returned my call immediately and said she could bring cars out for me to look at. What was I looking for in a car, she asked (hmm, Mike had not asked me that), and what else was I looking at? I told her: BMW, Lexus, Mercedes. "All three are great cars," she replied. "I have to admit, I personally love the Lexus line. Well, obviously— that's why I work here. But BMW and Mercedes are excellent cars, too. You'll do well either way." She offered to bring a car out for me to look at. The next day, she brought another. And then another. For the next week, Tink made sure I didn't pass a day without a Lexus to drive.

Finally, I got to Mercedes.

Like Tink, Ed at Mercedes wanted to know what else I was test-driving. When I said, "BMW—" he grunted. When I said ". . . and Lexus," he let out a snort of derision. "Not much of a car, really," Ed let me know, and he launched into a lecture about how many ways the Lexus was *not* what I wanted: it was basically a Camry body with an inflated price tag; I wouldn't be happy with a dealer so far away; he'd heard its airbag might not be safe . . . .

By the time I left the Mercedes dealership, Ed had *made the sale*: I got the Lexus.

Of course, there were features about the cars themselves that helped direct John's buying decision. But it was the attitudes of the three salespeople that clinched the deal.

When you tear down another, you are the one on whom it reflects most poorly. And when you take the high road and build up your competition, you create a rising tide that raises *all* the ships in the harbor—and that reflects quite well on you.

IV. The Law of Authenticity

The most valuable gift you have to offer is yourself.

21. Be Real

The speaker at that symposium had said, Add value. *I had nothing to add but myself. And apparently, that was exactly what'd been missing.*
— DEBRA DAVENPORT

It is not only your prospect who is a *person*: you are, too. You are *yourself*, and that is as it should be.

Let's clear up one of the most common misconceptions about sales: to touch people's lives, you do *not* need to be what is often called a "people person," that is, the bubbly, effervescent sort of personality who naturally and effortlessly connects, chats, and coffee-klatches with anyone and everyone. Or to put it more accurately, you don't need to be this kind of person *by nature*. Anyone can learn the dynamics of being great at sales, just as anyone can learn what it means to be a good friend.

You may have been taught that to be successful in sales, you need to "step outside your comfort zone." Let's reexamine that idea. If you push yourself to a place that makes you uncomfortable, chances are pretty good you'll end up making the other person uncomfortable, too. Consciously or not, they'll sense your discomfort—and attitudes are contagious.

We human beings tend to resist discomfort; in fact, we'll typically do anything to avoid putting ourselves in uncomfortable situations. Why base your entire career on something your strongest instincts tell you to avoid?

There is no need to seek discomfort; the world is already full of challenges, and it will throw plenty of discomfort your way.

Rather than try to leave your comfort zone, perhaps you can just be where you are—only *change* your comfort zone by stretching it a bit. Grow it, enlarge it, make it big enough to include the other person. Instead of stepping *out* of who you are, step *into* who you truly are.

When you observe great salespeople in action, do you see evidence of great discomfort? Not at all. Genuinely great salespeople make sales look easy. How? By stepping into who they are. They don't put on some artificial persona.

Bill Porter, the subject of the Emmy-winning 2002 movie *Door to Door*, is a living demonstration of the power of authenticity. Born with cerebral palsy, Porter was unable to find anyone who would hire him, but still he refused to go on disability. Despite his handicaps, which included slurred speech and a marked limp, he eventually persuaded the Watkins Company to give him a ten-mile door-to-door sales route.

He applied himself to his life in sales wholeheartedly, in the truest sense of the word. When a new potential customer answered the knock at their door, what they got was Bill Porter, the whole Bill Porter, and nothing but Bill Porter. He treated every customer with great care and respect, sending thank-you notes and following up scrupulously. In time he became the company's number one salesman. How? By *stepping into himself*.

Bill Porter refused to identify himself with his handicaps; consequently, others didn't feel sorry for him or pity him—they connected with him. He didn't merely deliver and service products for customers; he became part of their lives. He still does so today, at the age of seventy-six. "Although physically less active," Bill writes on his web site, "I still phone my long-time customers for their orders and to keep abreast of what is changing in their lives."

Some people have asked us, after reading about the Law of Authenticity in *The Go-Giver*, "How do I become authentic?" The truth is, authentic is not something you become; it's something you already are. Authenticity is not something you seek or take on, it's something you simply embrace.

Closely related to authenticity is the term *integrity*. Integrity means being whole, that is, not being divided. The word *integrity* comes from the Latin words *in* (not) and *tangere* (to touch), meaning untouched or pristine, something *in its original condition*.

Being whole means your words and actions are not separate things. When you do what you say, and say what you do, you are a man or a woman of your word.

There is a story about Gandhi (perhaps apocryphal) that is a beautiful example of the power of authenticity.

A woman once traveled a great distance to bring her son to see the famed spiritual and political leader. When they met, she said, "Bapu, please tell my child not to eat sugar." The great man asked her if she would please leave and come back with the child after thirty days. Irritated and confused, she agreed and left. A full month later she returned and brought her boy to see the man. Again she said, "We are back; it's been thirty days—please tell my child to stop eating sugar."

Gandhi tenderly looked at the boy and said, "My son, stop eating sugar." The boy agreed immediately, pledging that he would no longer eat sugar from that day forward.

Grateful but still confused, the mother said, "Bapu, I don't understand. Why did you make me leave and then journey all the way back here thirty days later, just so you could tell him what I asked you to tell him in the first place?"

Replied Gandhi, "Because thirty days ago, *I* was still eating sugar."

22. Present

Another wave of laughter and applause rushed through the place. "We're sixty seconds in, and she owns the room," Joe marveled to himself.

The word *present* can be read in several ways. You can read it as a verb: *to present*, to tell your story, explain your MacGuffin and all the marvelous things it can do for people. Or you can read it as an adjective, meaning "existing right now . . . having influence and being in the time and place at hand."

Which word do we mean here? Both. The secret to being effective when you *present* is to stay *present*.

In the old days, salespeople were trained to memorize facts, figures, and other information—to be a walking talking brochure. Giving information used to be a way of creating value. Not anymore. Today information is freely available. Giving people information doesn't give people value, it simply steals their time. Because of this, presenting is no longer about giving information (if it ever really was). It's about giving *meaning*.

The idea that becoming good at sales means learning how to be skilled at making a presentation is still the number one misconception about this business. The critical skill in your business is not your capacity to reel off facts and figures about your MacGuffin. It is your capacity to be *authentic*—to make a connection.

There is a saying in sales: *Facts tell, but stories sell*. This is easy to remember because it rhymes, but it's not entirely true. Stories don't necessarily sell. What they do is *connect*.

Depending on what kind of selling you do, you may give formal presentations to groups large or small; or your presentations may happen on the phone, over coffee, or face-to-face in an office, or in living rooms. But it doesn't matter where or in what context; the same principles apply.

Let's take the example of a formal presentation. Jack has been asked to speak to a local organization about the service he represents. After being introduced by the host, Jack steps to the center of the stage and looks out tentatively at the group.

> Hel—hello? [Looks around, taps his lapel mike.] Am I on? Can you hear me? Good. Okay . . . wow, what a great-looking group! Hey, I can't tell you how excited I am to be here with you tonight. Before I go any further, I just want to thank Jim Jenkins for putting this together—everyone, give Jim a hand!

There's scattered applause, a few people coughing, much shifting in seats—and just like that, before he's even really gotten started, poor Jack's presentation is essentially over:

from here on, nobody in the room is really going to hear a word he says. Why not? Because the saying is true: you only get one chance to make a first impression—and Jack wasted those precious first moments focused on himself. He was not *present*.

Every time you open your mouth to speak, you are responding to a question in your mind. Here are the questions Jack's opening is responding to:

How do I look? What should I say? How am I doing? Does it show that I'm nervous? Will they like me?

Jack's heart is in the right place, and he does have something of value he genuinely wants to share with this group. But asking himself the wrong questions has led to this kind of gosh-I'm-excited, breaking-the-ice opening riff that 99 percent of poor presenters use to open their talks.

And the percentage of *great* presenters who start their talks this way? Zero. Why, because they're polished, skilled, have nerves of steel? No, it's because truly great presenters know how to take their focus completely off themselves.

When a great presenter faces her audience, here are the kinds of questions she asks herself:

What do these people want most? Who are they? What are they searching for? Why are they here? And what is the single most valuable thing I could possibly convey to them?

Let's do that little talk again, only this time Jack will remind himself before the meeting begins that this is not about him—it's about them. He puts himself in his audience's shoes, asks himself what are their fears, what are their hopes, what might he have to offer them that would give them the greatest value.

Here's how Jack's presentation starts this time. After being introduced, he steps to center stage, stands straight, gazes directly at his audience, and begins:

> I still remember how it felt, the time it happened to me. It was twenty-three years ago. I was young, ambitious—and nervous. I was nervous because I'd been summoned into the boss's office, and when I got there I heard those nine terrifying words I never want to hear again in my life: "*Jack, I'm sorry—we've had to make some cutbacks . . .*"

There is not a sound in the place. Nobody moves. All eyes are riveted on Jack and every soul in the room is hanging on his every word. Why, because he's such a polished speaker? No, it's not polished: it's *authentic*—and Jack has not wasted a single second of the group's precious time and attention but has gone right to the heart of something that could be vitally important to the people sitting in front of him.

Of course you want to have a firm grasp of your informational key points, product benefits, vignettes, and anecdotes you might share . . . but relax. You will not be graded on how well you've mastered delivery of this information. What you will be graded on is the quality of the interaction. Bring yourself to each conversation with these questions:

Who is this person? What do they want? What are they searching for? What is the single most valuable thing I could possibly offer them?

And remind yourself: it's not about you, it's about them.

"What about scripts?" we are often asked. "Is it inauthentic to have words and phrases memorized?"

We don't know anyone who is moved to tears or touched deeply by a canned pitch read word for word over the phone by a telemarketer. But that doesn't mean scripts and memorized phrases cannot be expressions of authenticity, whether they come from company materials or you write them yourself.

Think for a moment of your favorite musician, popular or classical. Picture them performing that Bach solo or singing that song onstage with their band. Do you suppose they've memorized that music ahead of time? Of course they have—every note and every word. Is it authentic? Some would say listening to a great musician perform is just about the most authentic experience there is.

Authenticity doesn't mean you can't use preplanned words. It just means that when you do, you have to make them your own, in both your head and your heart.

23. Undersell

"I've sold a few more homes since then," she began, and an appreciative wave of laughter went through the audience. Everyone present knew Debra Davenport's sales record. "A few more homes" was probably the understatement of the decade.

People often think of sales as a business of convincing other people to do what you want them to do. Great salespeople never try to convince anyone of anything.

The effort to convince contains within itself the seeds of its own undoing. The word *convince* derives from the Latin *vincere*, meaning "to conquer." To convince means "to overcome in argument." "A man convinced against his will," said Dale Carnegie, "is of the same opinion still." And really, is there any other way to be convinced than against your will?

"Believe me . . . Trust me . . . Take it from me . . . If you want *my* opinion . . ." If you notice these phrases appearing in your language, we recommend you ferret them out and eliminate them. None of them is effective at conveying genuine value. First off, they are all me-focused. More important, they are the kind of forceful assertions that cast long shadows of doubt in the mind of the listener. If the speaker is genuinely trustworthy, does he need to tell us that?

What about this one:

> This MacGuffin is *incredible*. It's *unbelievable*—I'm telling you, it's the best MacGuffin ever made! You are going to love it—in fact, once you have one, you'll say you don't know how you ever got along without it!

It's almost hard to count the number of ways this paragraph offends the listener and puts up barriers instead of making connections. (And by the way, the words *incredible* and *unbelievable* both literally mean "don't believe what I'm saying"—not the most effective way to build trust.)

What all these expressions have in common is that they *oversell*.

There is a wonderful expression in sales: *It's better to underpromise and overdeliver than the other way around*. This is an excellent way of stating the Law of Value, and it's the core philosophy of great salesmanship: *Follow through on your promises—every one of them*. It applies to everything, from always being on time for appointments (whether in person or on the phone), to sending that bit of information or link or reference that you said you'd send, to delivering the kind of every-time, never-miss customer service that helped make Bill Porter famous.

Hype is the ultimate oversell. The worst thing about hype is that by definition it is impossible to fulfill its promise.

Hype and overselling almost invariably achieve the opposite of their intended goal. They make people want to back away, turn around, and run.

Of course, most salespeople do not resort to hype on purpose. They have been taught to display enthusiasm, and they truly do believe in their MacGuffin's benefits. But forced or rampant enthusiasm often ends up looking and sounding like hype, or its cousin, bravado.

Beneath bravado there often lurks a hidden core of ambivalence, doubt, and insecurity, and even though it's hidden, people sense it clearly. After all, if you were genuinely sure of yourself and your MacGuffin, you wouldn't have to resort to all this bluster.

We're not suggesting you tamp down your enthusiasm, hide your genuine excitement for your products, or keep your passion under a bushel. Not at all. But there are two classes of positive declaration. There is the forceful assertion, and then there is the simple statement of fact that springs from the quiet stillness of authenticity. The first is born from bravado, the effort to appear confident; the second, from the realm of simple knowing.

It's much like the wisdom in Gandhi's enormously popular aphorism, "You must *be* the change you wish to see in the world." Confidence and genuine enthusiasm are not missiles that work only when they are launched at others; they are lights that glow from within.

At one point in his career, John was recommended by some mutual friends to a well-established author as a possible ghostwriter for a project under serious deadline. The author had expressed hesitation at the fee John quoted, and a conference call was organized between the various parties.

As the call began, the author's first words to John threw down a gauntlet: "So, are you half as good as they say you are?"

John replied: "Yes, sir—I am exactly one half as good as they say!"

The man roared with laughter, hired John to do the writing—and after the work was done, paid him exactly *twice* the requested fee.

Underpromise. Overdeliver.

24. Listen

I can't remember ever feeling so . . . so listened *to. So* heard.

—SUSAN

When people use the term *communication skills*, they're often thinking about the ability to express ourselves well through what we say, which might more accurately be called *expression* skills. But expressing yourself is only one half of the communication process—one half at best. The real secret of great communicators is not their talk but their empathy: before they open their mouths, they have a clear grasp of their audience's experience.

And there is only one sure way to arrive at that clear grasp: listening.

The greater half of communication skills lies not in what you say or even how you say it, but in how well you hear what the other person says.

In our busy, fast-paced world, genuine listening is rare. Most of the time we listen in a way you could describe as *listening in order to . . .* in order to what? In order to get to the end of *their* sentence so I can make *my* point. In order to get information that will help me make the sale. In order to find an opening where I can jump in and say, "Ah, yes, I know *exactly* what you mean! And you know, my product would be the *perfect* solution to that dilemma!"

Great salespeople don't listen *in order to* anything. They simply listen. They listen because they are interested in the other person; they are curious. They want to know the person. They listen to learn.

There is a technique sometimes taught in sales called "active listening," the idea being that you make the other person feel more heard if you engage more actively in the process, giving them regular feedback—nodding, saying "uh-huh," and so forth—and when they're finished, repeating back what you think the person just said to make sure you heard it right.

There's value in the idea, and it's certainly well intended. But in practice it too often misses the mark. Like the teaching that tells us to use the other person's name often, this can become irritatingly artificial. "Uh-huh, right, yes, I know just whatcha mean, yes, uh-huh, yeah, yeah, uh-huh"—*stop, please*. All that "feedback" gets in the way of listening.

The more sincere and respectful way to listen is to *simply listen*.

How you listen depends on what questions you are asking yourself. You can listen from a context that says, "What do I think about what this person is saying, and how am I going to respond when they're finished?" Or you can listen from a context that simply says, "What exactly is this person saying?"

The problem with the first is that your focus is not on what the person is saying, but on what you are going to say back—which generally means that you're not really hearing what the person is saying. In the second case you're focusing on the other person, and trusting that when it's your turn to respond, you'll simply do that.

Ninety-nine percent of what looks like listening in the world is not genuine listening, it's just waiting at a stoplight with the mind's engine running until the light turns green and we can go again. When you listen, put it in NEUTRAL; even better, put it in PARK and shut off the engine. Just listen.

Our friend Gilles Arbour tells a story about his early days in network marketing. After explaining his opportunity to a prospect, the man said, "You mean, it's like Amway?"

Oh no, no, Gilles hastened to assure the man. That is, yes, it was the same *general* idea, but no, in this way and that way and these other ways, it was really *nothing* like Amway.

"That's too bad," replied the man. "I *like* Amway."

Don't *assume* you know what the other person means by what he just said—because you don't, at least not unless you ask.

One of the powerful things about listening is that it is often the only way to really get to the heart of the matter. People often don't voice their real thoughts and concerns right away. In fact, people often don't know what their real thoughts and concerns *are*, at least not at first.

The truth, as Plato taught, is revealed in dialogue, and listening is what allows a conversation to blossom into genuine dialogue. However, when you don't really listen, a conversation can easily devolve into a sparring match.

For example, let's suppose you are in real estate, and you are talking with a potential buyer about a house you just showed her.

BUYER: I don't know . . . I think maybe the house is too far from town.

YOU: Actually, it's only ten miles away, not really far at all.

BUYER: Well . . . we like to feel really close to where everything is.

YOU: Not a problem! It's a twenty-five-minute ride on a bad day—without traffic, you can make it in fifteen.

BUYER: I don't know, I'm not sure . . .

YOU: But you like the home itself, right?

This isn't communication; this is arm wrestling. Once you start, it's over, because even if you win, you lose. Let's try this again, and this time, let's *listen*.

BUYER: I don't know . . . I think maybe the house is too far from town.

YOU: How so? What are you thinking?

BUYER: Well . . . you know we *love* the home. But we like to feel really close to where everything is.

YOU: Sounds like that's really important to you. So, when you say "where everything is," are there specific things you're thinking of?

BUYER: Well, yeah. I guess, with our little girl, and maybe a few more kids coming over the next couple years, we want to make sure we always have access to whatever we need, whether it's just something like shopping or going to the movies—or, Heaven forbid, if one of the kids hurts herself and we have to get to the hospital fast . . . My husband and I both grew up right in the city and we're used to being just minutes from everything. I guess, to us, ten miles seems like a lifetime away.

YOU: That makes a lot of sense. So, as much as you love the idea of living in this home, we need to balance that with your and Dave's comfort level as far as distance from town goes. Do I have that right?

BUYER: Yes, exactly. That's *exactly* it!

YOU: You know, I'm wondering . . . there are some development plans under way right now just a couple miles from here. I understand there'll be stores, a movie theater, even an emergency center. I don't know if what's coming there will be enough to meet your family's needs, but would you be open to taking a look at it and seeing if we're even in the ballpark?

By listening instead of debating, and *communicating* that you were listening, you have advanced the sales process. Why? Because you have conveyed to your buyer that your goal is to create value for her, and not just to make a sale. Rather than denying her perspective and trying to convince her that her concerns aren't valid, which is what happened in the first example, you have honored her perspective.

That is the ultimate benefit of genuine listening: you honor the other person. You let them know that they are important and that you value them. And that is the bedrock of a great relationship.

In fact, chances are very good that the person you're listening to has nobody else in their life who listens to them the way you are doing.

There is a turning point in *The Go-Giver*, almost exactly halfway through the story. This is the moment when Joe first begins to genuinely grasp the lesson his teachers are showing him, and the situation in which he has this glimpse has nothing at all to do with business. In fact, it is the only point in the story when we see Joe at home with his wife, Susan.

For the first time in their relationship, Joe sets aside his own concerns and listens wholeheartedly, with no agenda, while Susan pours her heart out talking about her difficult day at work. He moves from a fifty-fifty perspective to what Sam calls "a one hundred percent" perspective.

The shift he makes is quiet and undramatic—indeed, even as it happens Joe himself thinks he has failed utterly to be of any help at all. But without this shift, the rest of the story could not have unfolded and Joe would likely have gone on to live what Thoreau so famously called a life of quiet desperation.

Instead, his entire life transforms.

What happens in that critical moment? He listens.

25. Objections

"All this giving stuff sounds great—for some people. For people like me, maybe, or Nicole, or Ernesto. But not for you. It's just not who you are." There was a moment of silence. *"Is that how it is?"*

Joe sighed. *"Something like that,"* he admitted.

Now we come to the nitty-gritty moment of the sales process, the point salespeople often dread most: dealing with "objections." And just as with most every other aspect of the sales process, the Go-Giver's approach here may seem almost upside down from what you have heard before.

As we unwrap this process, we'll discover something wonderful: this is often the very moment that offers the greatest opportunity to create value for the other person. In fact, here is where we encounter one of the most powerful and least understood secrets of sales:

Dealing with what most people call "objections" is often the point in the process when the sale really happens.

The natural impulse upon getting an objection is to *counter* it. In other words, when you sense that another person has an issue, concern, criticism, or hesitation about your MacGuffin, you suit up and prepare to do battle. The typical approach to "overcoming objections" is essentially a type of warfare. No wonder people feel like flinching, wincing, or running when it's done to them.

The truth about objections is that most of the time, *they aren't really objections*.

Put yourself in the other person's shoes. You know all about your MacGuffin; you are an expert in everything about your MacGuffin. But the other person is not; they are just now considering it, possibly for the very first time. They also have a lot going on in their lives. Who knows what issues of their own are nagging for attention in the backs of their minds, even while the two of you are talking?

The point the other person actually puts into words is probably not the totality of what they're really thinking. In fact, chances are excellent that they aren't quite sure just *what* they think—and in the effort to clarify their own position, they seize on the first thought that comes to mind and toss it out to you as a way of saying, "Hang on, not so fast."

In a very real sense, what they end up deciding they really *do* think depends on you and *how you treat them in the next thirty seconds*. You can do one of two things. You can challenge them, which will probably harden their thoughts into a firm negative position. Or you can reframe their point as a request for clarification (which is what it really is)—and join them as a partner in the process.

The Go-Giver's approach to another person's objection

is empathy: instead of facing off and staking out a debate position, step over to where the person is standing, stand next to them, and look at their objection *with* them.

We sometimes describe this as *turning in the direction of the skid*.

When you first learned to ride a bike, what did they teach you about falling? When you feel yourself falling, turn the wheel *in the same direction*, stopping the fall. But your young, untrained instinct screamed, "No, the other way, turn the other way! You're falling *right*—turn *left*. Cut it hard!" And what happened when you followed that instinct? You ended up on the pavement, on your butt, wondering what just happened.

Communicating with people works exactly the same way. When your conversation feels like it hits a bump and you might be losing your balance, your instinct tells you, *Turn the other way! Cut it hard!*

OTHER PERSON: I don't know, this product seems pretty expensive—

YOU: Expensive?! Not at all, really, when you consider what you're getting here, it's worth every penny and more—and hey, have you ever added up how much you spend each month on sodas, snacks, and junk food?

Crash, right on your butt.

You encountered the same concept when you first learned how to drive a car. "When you find yourself on an icy road," your teacher said, "and you start going into a skid, *turn in the direction of the skid*." It seemed completely nonsensical, and every fiber in your being told you, "No, the other way, turn *away* from the skid!"—but anyone who has driven on icy roads knows that your teacher was absolutely correct.

Precisely the same thing applies in your conversations. When the conversation hits an ice patch, turn *in the direction of the skid*.

OTHER PERSON: I don't know, this product seems pretty expensive.

YOU: So, you're saying *x* dollars seems like a lot to invest in a MacGuffin?

OTHER PERSON: Well, yeah.

YOU: Certainly something to consider. If I may ask, what kind of results would you need to see to justify that kind of price?

It's a matter of turning your wheel in the same direction the other person is going—not trying to force them back the other way.

This does not mean you necessarily agree with the objection itself. Saying, "Certainly something to consider" or "I get what you're saying" is not the same thing as saying, "You're right—this product *is* expensive!"

It's not that you have to agree with the person's *point*; it's a matter of *being with the person*—not jousting or dueling with them. Of trusting yourself and the facts about your product enough to not have to push. It shows the other person—and yourself—that you're not afraid of questions.

It may feel awkward or strange at first, like you'll never get the hang of it. But as with riding a bike, you will—and once you do, you'll never forget it.

By the way, this principle holds true in all relationships, not just in sales. When your spouse or your best friend says something you take as critical, what's your instinct? *Turn the other way!* Deflect, defend, resist. And what happens?

> SPOUSE: Honey, there's something we need to talk about. I'm worried that you're starting to get too wrapped up in work and not spending enough time at home.
>
> YOU: That's just not true—we spent the *whole afternoon* together Saturday. And you *know* what challenges I'm facing at work these days—and I'm only doing this for our future . . .

There you go, smack down on the pavement. Instead, go with it: turn in the direction of the skid.

> SPOUSE: Honey, there's something we need to talk about. I'm worried that you're starting to get too wrapped up in work and not spending enough time at home.
>
> YOU: Really, I'm doing that? I had no idea. Wow.
>
> SPOUSE: Yeah, well it just seems like it, lately.
>
> YOU: What do think we could be doing differently?

You see what happened here? You've joined with the person to look at their point from the same side of the table. This is the key to Go-Giver sales: always be on the same side. Sales is not something you do *to* another person, it's something you do *with* that person.

In fact, as we said at the start of this chapter, what salespeople usually call *objections* often present the clearest opportunities to create value for the other person.

How? By honoring their point or concern. When you say, "That's a great question" or "That's a good point" and then join with them to examine the issue they raised, you let them know it's welcome and appreciated. But here's the thing: those are only effective things to say if they're *true*. It's not enough to just *tell* the person they're making a great point. The only way you can say that authentically is if *you genuinely see it as a great point*.

Ah, and that's the beauty of it: it *is*. You don't necessarily agree with the objection, but it's a great point because it is *their* point. And not only is it a great point: as we said above, it will very possibly be the moment when the sale really happens.

You may not *see* it happen; the other person may not be aware of it in the moment. And it may take many more minutes of conversation, even one or more additional conversations in the future, before the actual transaction occurs. But make no mistake about it, this is often the moment—the point when they have entrusted you with their uncertainties, doubts, fears, and hesitations, and you have honored and embraced them rather than butting up against them—when the connection is solidified and the sale itself begins to show up.

Years ago, when Bob was in the business of selling radio advertising, he called on a woman who owned an exterminating company. Almost before he had gotten started, she slammed the door of an objection in his face.

As soon as I introduced myself, she stopped me right away: "Sorry, we don't have advertising in our budget."

"That's fine," I said, "I completely understand. I don't want to take any more of your time. May I ask you something?" And I asked her a question about how her service worked. I was genuinely curious: here was a woman who spent all her time figuring out how to thwart insects. What was that like, I wondered, and how did she do it?

She began explaining her work, and the more she talked the more fascinated I became. This woman knew more about the lives, diets, mating habits, and behaviors of insects than the entomology department of an entire university!

As she talked on, I also learned she was a grandmother who adored her grandchildren, and that she had a passion for helping make homes clean and safe for the families that lived in them.

I really didn't want to impose, but it was hard to tear myself away. Finally I got up to leave, and she abruptly asked, "So, how much is your introductory package?"

A little bewildered, I quoted her our normal price. She bought it right then and there.

Bob gave no resistance to her objection, and certainly never "asked for the order" or got to the point of making a "close." He didn't have to. She talked herself right past her own objection and "closed" herself.

26. The "Close"

Well, let's see . . . There was the Assumptive Close, the Bonus Close, the Concession Close, the Distraction Close, the Emotion Close, the Future Close, the Golden Gate Bridge Close, the Humor Close, the IQ Close, the Jersey City Close, the Kill Clause Close, the Leveraged Asset Close, the Money's-Not-Everything Close, the Now-or-Never Close, the Ownership Close, the Puppy Dog Close, the Quality Close, the Reversal Close, the Standing-Room-Only Close, the Takeaway Close, the Underpriced-Value Close, the Vanity Close, the Window-of-Opportunity Close, the Xaviera Hollander Close, Ya-Ya Sisterhood Close and Zsa Zsa Gabor Close! Honey, I learned how to close! —DEBRA DAVENPORT

"This all sounds well and good—" our skeptic is back, and he has an objection "—but doesn't there come a point when you have to actually ask for the sale? After all, sales aren't going to just happen by themselves!"

He has a point. You do arrive at the place where the two of you have talked long enough about your MacGuffin and it may be time for a buying decision. There will be those rare moments when the other person will come right out and say, "Okay, look, I'm sold, I want to get this right now—

what works better for you, a Visa or a personal check?" But most of the time, you need to ask the question.

Classic sales training teaches us all sorts of approaches to this moment, creating scenarios that we run over and over in our heads. But these can end up feeling like exactly what they are: techniques. People can sense they're being "closed," and it doesn't feel good.

And it's not just how it makes the other person feel; there's also how it makes *you* feel. The moment we start using a *closing technique*, it's easy for the process to start being about *me and my results* instead of about the other person. In fact, we get queasy about "popping the question" only when our focus is on ourselves:

How am I doing? Am I doing this right? Do I sound natural? How does that closing technique go again? And is that the one I should be using here, or wait! Should I maybe be using that other one? How will I feel if they say no—and how will that reflect on me?

It's funny how squeamish we can get about this stage of the process. It's almost as if we were asking out our first date, or practicing exactly what to say when we ask that special girl or guy if they'll go to the prom with us. But we're no longer in high school, and this is not the prom.

If we instead keep our focus on the other person, then our question comes from a place of authentic asking. Is this what the other person wants? Would this be of genuine value to them? The simplest way to ask is the simplest way to ask:

Jack, are you at a point where you'd like to go ahead and purchase?

or,

Jack, would you like to buy one of these MacGuffins?

If Jack says yes, then that's that—but what if he hesitates or isn't sure? This is where the traditional sales process might step up the effort to close the prospect. But that approach is aimed at *making the sale*, while our goal is always to *create value*. We want to create a process that includes the other person, not one that confronts the other person. So rather than focus here on *closing*, we like to focus on *opening*.

Even in the best of situations, when you come to the point of purchase, chances are good the other person is feeling some degree of pressure, even if it's only self-imposed. After all, they are in the process of making a decision. All buying decisions of any significant amount are emotional decisions, and with an emotional decision there inevitably comes a feeling of pressure.

That pressure is exacerbated when we feel we don't have a choice, so we naturally react by looking for a way to exercise our prerogative to make a choice. When faced with greater pressure in the sales process, the natural response is to look for any type of escape or excuse that allows us to say no. After all, "no" almost always feels safer than "yes." Thus:

pressure → need for escape → *no*

is followed by a big internal sigh of relief: *Ahh, I'm no longer boxed into a corner*. This is why pressuring someone for a purchasing decision is usually the surest way to maneuver them into saying no. And even if they do say yes, they will feel resentful about it, certainly never refer you to others, and perhaps even eventually rescind the sale itself.

There are two things you can do to serve the other person here. First, *apply no pressure*. Zero. None. And second, as a way of honoring the possibility that they may be feeling the urge to seek an escape route, *provide one*. When the point of decision arrives, rather than trying to corner them or hem them *in*, voluntarily give them an *out*.

Instead of trying to close the prospect, *open* the dialogue to more possibilities.

To get a sense of what this might look like, let's step outside this moment-of-decision sales situation for a moment and look at an example in a different context.

Let's say you're trying to reach someone important, perhaps a decision maker in an organization—maybe this person is your ultimate customer, someone you want to talk with about possible company purchases, or is an important connection you'd like to make—and right now you've gotten as far as the person's assistant.

To make things interesting, let's also say this assistant is determined to block your access to the person you want to see.

You've been on the phone for five minutes, have carefully explained what you're looking for and why it's a very reasonable request, and he hasn't budged. You've responded instead of reacting; you've stayed totally polite; you've gone in the direction of the skid when he gave you his objections (his reasons why it was "impossible" to talk with his boss); and you have just reframed your request in the most agreeable terms. You know your conversation is nearly over—so before he replies, you add what Bob likes to call the Eight Key Words:

If you can't do it, I'll definitely understand.

There is a palpable pause on the other end of the line. This time, when he speaks up, his tone has changed. "I don't know," he begins, "I . . . I'll see what I can do."

What happened? Instead of bullying him into a corner, where the only way he could save face would be to exercise his authority and turn down your request, you have saved face *for* him. Instead of trying to *close* him, you've *opened* the process.

And the degree to which you give the other person an escape hatch is the degree to which they will be less likely to feel the need to use it.

Now, back to your potential customer and the moment-of-purchase decision. You've asked Jack if he'd like to make a purchase, and he's hesitating or starting to balk. He's feeling the pressure of the emotional decision he's facing. So you open up the process, which can be as simple as saying:

Jack, this may or may not be for you.

"Aha," says the traditionally trained salesperson, "I get it—this is like a *takeaway close*, right? You say, 'Well, Jack, this may not be the right MacGuffin for you'—and then, because you're pulling it away, he'll actually be more likely to jump at it? Clever!"

No, this is *not* a takeaway close. This isn't any kind of close at all: it's an *open*. And we're not saying anything *in order to* get Jack to do any specific thing. We're saying it to help take the pressure off, so he can feel more relaxed about making the right decision for him. And whether that decision is to buy our MacGuffin, or not to buy it, or to postpone making any decision at all, is entirely up to him.

Remember that our underlying goal here is to create value for the other person.

As with objections, this may at times feel counterintuitive. It may feel like you're giving the other person an "out" and relinquishing control of the process. That's because you are. You're treating Jack as a partner in the process rather than as a passive subject. And if this feels a little strange at first, don't worry: you'll quickly get a feel for it.

What's more, it feels great, both to you and to the other person—because it puts you together on the same side of the question. It is another way of turning in the direction of the skid.

27. Silence

He stopped moving and listened to the quiet stillness in the normally busy office. What was it he was feeling? The quiet felt almost as if it were alive. Motionless, but listening. It felt . . . how would you describe it? Receptive.

The legendary architect and futurist Buckminster ("Bucky") Fuller hit a deep crisis in his twenties. Having gone broke and lost his infant daughter to meningitis, he felt his life was a shambles. Standing on the edge of Lake Michigan on a bitter winter evening, about to throw himself in, he paused to think. His life was a mess, he reasoned, because he had spent his years up to that point repeating things other people had told him.

In that moment, Bucky decided to close his mouth and not open it again until he was sure that the words he spoke really came *from him*.

For the next two years, he did not utter a single word. When he finally did begin to speak again, what came out was not always easy for people to understand, but the passion and conviction were unmistakably and unequivocally

his and nobody else's. Over the years, people came to recognize that his words also contained great genius.

What happened to Bucky is available to each and every
one of us, and it was simply this: in his silence, he discovered his authentic self.

Earlier we mentioned the critical turning point for Joe
in *The Go-Giver*. This is what happened to him, too: it was
in those minutes of being entirely silent and fully listening
to his wife, Susan, that he began to understand the laws of
the Go-Giver.

You tap into your greatest value and authenticity when
you are not speaking. It's not that what you say isn't important. That's just not where your power lies.

The most common way inexperienced salespeople shoot
themselves in the foot is by *saying too much* when they talk
about their product or service. Why do they say too much?
Because they don't yet really trust themselves. True conviction is best conveyed not through more words but through
fewer; it dwells *behind* the words.

The Bill of Rights is stated in 660 words. Lincoln's Gettys-
burg Address consists of 267 words. The Ten Commandments
takes 163. (And that's in English; in Hebrew it's only 77.)

It doesn't take a lot of words to make a powerful point.
Say less; communicate more.

In conversation, often the most powerful moments are
not when you are speaking but when you pause and make
room for the other person. Sometimes we rush to fill in
those empty moments, perhaps out of fear that the silence
will feel awkward. But it's better to let the silences be there:
silences in a conversation have a wonderful way of coaxing
deeper thoughts to the surface.

The most important words that will ever pass between you and your prospective customers are the words spoken by them—not by you.

What you have most to offer others, you have to offer least of all through what you say, in greater part through what you do, but in greatest part through who you *are*.

V. The Law of Receptivity

*The key to effective giving
is to stay open to receiving.*

28. Stay Open

At this instant, all over the globe, all of humanity is breathing in oxygen and breathing out carbon dioxide. So is the rest of the animal kingdom. And right now, at this instant, all over the globe, the billions and billions of organisms of the plant kingdom are doing the exact opposite—they're breathing in carbon dioxide and breathing out oxygen. Their giving is our receiving, and our giving is their receiving.   —PINDAR

"The first four laws felt to me like polished wood," one interviewer told us after reading *The Go-Giver*, "but the fifth law? That one gave me splinters."

Many readers have told us that the Law of Receptivity was the hardest of the Five Laws for them to accept and put into practice personally. This is important to note, because while the first four laws are not about the sale itself (they are all about *giving*), the fifth law *is* about the sale. This is the part where you actually *receive*.

And for many, this is not as easy at it sounds. Think back to the last time someone paid you a compliment. How did you receive it?

In chapter 4, we mentioned the treacherous dichotomy that runs so deep in our culture: the idea that we can be big-hearted and generous *or* look out for ourselves, but not do both at once—that there is an inherent contradiction between self-interest and altruism. Here is how Nicole Martin describes it:

> I was brought up with a belief that there are two types of people in the world. There are people who *get rich*, and there are people who *do good*. My belief system said you're one or the other, you can't be both.

A review that appeared a few weeks after *The Go-Giver* was released offered a vivid example of just how deep this belief system runs even in our sophisticated world. The reviewer summed up the book this way:

> Through Pindar, Joe meets and learns from a number of successful business people who share their secret: It's better to give than to receive.

This is fascinating when you consider Pindar's actual words as they appear in the book itself:

> It's not *better* to give than to receive. It's *insane* to try to give and *not* receive!

This fundamental conviction—that giving is *good* and receiving is, if not *bad*, at least *less good*—is so ingrained that this intelligent, literate, professional reviewer came away with a message that directly contradicts the very words on the page.

Whether or not we are aware of it, there is often a part of us that silently disapproves of, and even actively resists, our receiving. And nowhere does this insidious self-sabotage do more damage than in sales.

If you cannot accept a compliment gracefully; if you resist asking for what you need from those close to you; if you feel awkward, guilty, or somehow undeserving when good things are handed to you by others, then it should come as no surprise that when it comes to *receiving a sale*, your inner inclination may be to balk at the gift.

If you do not feel naturally graceful about receiving this sale from the other person, then you will bring that feeling of discomfort to the sales process itself. Often this surfaces as a sense of the transaction being forced or uneasy. You can seek to remedy this discomfort through the use of formulas and techniques, but you and the other person will both still sense the underlying unease. At best, it will discolor the experience and put a damper on future exchanges with this person; at worst, it can sabotage the sale itself.

The problem, as Joe eventually realizes, is that "if you don't let yourself receive, you're refusing the gifts of others—and you shut down the flow."

And that flow is exactly what your business is all about. That flow is the goal and purpose of sales and selling. In the world of biology, it expresses itself through the exchange of oxygen and carbon dioxide; in the world of sales, it expresses itself through the exchange of products, services, value, and money. But it's the same flow in either case. It is breathing; it is *life*.

In the spring of 2009, four young social-marketing entrepreneurs from Chicago—Gilbert Melott, Gabe Strom, Brian Tomkins, and Bradley Will—decided to take *The Go-Giver's* message on the road, driving the thousand-plus miles from Chicago to Orlando to attend an event Bob was hosting.

Calling their trip the Go-Giver Tour, the four planned to stop at campuses in major cities along the way to attend "Tweetups," local meetings of Twitter aficionados. Says Gilbert:

> Our goal was to popularize the message of *The Go-Giver* among young entrepreneurs and challenge them to use it to increase their own level of success.

Along the way, they would provide coaching and mentoring to the young entrepreneurs who accompanied them, and expose them to a range of situations and circumstances. The four entrepreneurs produced a video on the topic, announcing that they would award open seats in their vehicles as prizes to those who submitted the best "Go-Giver testimonial videos" to add to their production.

Their vision had one major challenge: money.

> We could see that the trip was going to take a pretty substantial budget. We wanted to include as many people as possible, because we believed that the five laws are crucial to the success of young leaders—but the more people we included and the longer we stretched the trip, the more our costs would escalate.

Without a clear plan for raising the money, they forged ahead and began using Internet-driven social media to let people know what they were doing. Soon they were flooded with comments, questions, and requests—one of the most common being, "How can I help?"

People wanted to contribute time, energy, and money to the tour. At first we were uncomfortable with the idea of accepting help, especially monetary help. So we decided we needed to revisit the Law of Receptivity.

Some supporters donated money for the group's lodging, others for gas and tolls. Video editors and web designers contributed their time; a printing company donated magnets with the slogan, ARE YOU GOING TO BE A GIVER OR A TAKER TODAY? Another vendor created GET YOUR GIVE ON! T-shirts, and when their T-shirt sponsor fell through another quickly stepped forward.

But the biggest surprise had to do with our vehicles. We knew we were collecting a pretty sizable group for this thousand-mile trip; none of us owned vans or buses, and we didn't see how we would be able to afford to rent them for the duration.

And then, out of the blue, they were contacted by Ford Motor Company.

Ford had somehow noticed what we were doing and wanted to help! They said they regularly work with the Social Media Group to provide vehicles to journalists—and in our case, they decided to stretch the definition of "journalist." They provided us with two 2009 Ford vehicles to take us across the country as we spread the book's message.

Ford asked for nothing in return, nor did the dozens of individuals who rallied around the four to support their enterprise. They simply *gave*—and in a way, they almost could not have helped doing so. The four young entrepreneurs had made themselves *receptive*.

Here is the heart of the matter: we have learned to view giving and receiving, altruism and self-interest, as two conflicting and contradictory states, at odds with each other, the one noble and the other selfish. But this is not how the genuinely successful see it, nor is it how they live their lives.

The genuinely successful view living with generosity as an integral part of creating success, not as something that comes *out of* success or that you can begin doing only *after* you've become successful—and they see receiving as an integral part of generosity. They eagerly receive, delight in the receiving—and just as eagerly pass it on. They don't stop the flow, they *join in* with the flow.

To be genuinely successful, we need to *allow* ourselves to receive.

One way to develop this inclination is to practice *appreciation*. All religions and traditional schools of thought counsel the wisdom of vigilant appreciation, sometimes popularly referred to as an *attitude of gratitude*. "Count your blessings," we were told as children.

The tradition of prayer, also rich in so many different

cultures throughout the world, generally comes in two aspects: there is the prayer of *petition*, where we ask for something, and the prayer of *appreciation*, the heartfelt expression of thankful acceptance for what we already have or hope to receive. The latter is especially powerful—because it evokes the Law of Receptivity.

Counting your blessings, sitting quietly at the end of a busy day, and practicing heartfelt appreciation—these are acts of voluntary receptivity.

Gratitude helps to ensure, as Pindar might have said, that you're "facing in the right direction." Clothe every action in a garment of gratitude for the myriad blessings that exist in your life right now, right at this moment, and you will be nourishing rather than crimping the flow.

In truth, we each receive all manner of gifts, constantly and throughout the day. Genuine Go-Givers do not focus *only* on giving: they are also intensely aware of the gifts they receive. Indeed, they *delight* in the gifts they receive. And that is why they continue to receive so much.

Bob tells a story about an encounter with his book-keeper, Trina, who had come to the office to work on their books for the month. Stepping into the office for a moment, Bob happened to notice the pen Trina was using. Here's how Bob tells it:

> It wasn't an especially fancy or expensive pen, but I liked its design and told her so. I asked her where she bought it. She replied, "Oh, here, take this one, I've got plenty of them."
>
> "I can't take your pen," I said.
>
> She asked, "Why not?"

"Because it's your pen."

"So what?" she asked. "I'm giving it to you."

"No," I countered, "I wouldn't feel right taking it."

Trina narrowed her eyes, looked straight at me, and said: "Bob, it's a very simple two-step process. One, take the pen. Two, say *thank you*."

It's so easy to forget—and yet, once you've practiced it a bit, so easy to *do*.

Sometimes you simply have to take the pen and say *thank you*.

29. Left Field

The phone rang. Joe swiveled to stare at it, then at the wall clock. At six-fifteen? On a Friday?

What is so interesting about giving is not only that it pays, but that it pays in such unexpected ways. When you live with generosity, blessings come to you from corners and avenues you never would have expected.

There is the world that we see: the people, events, and circumstances we're paying attention to, the things we are aware of and can track logically. And then there is a whole other, vastly larger area of the universe, an area we'll call *left field*, which includes the 99.9 percent that we're *not* paying attention to or noticing at all, the realm of events and circumstances that we cannot possibly trace and that transcend our capacity to comprehend cause and effect. This uncharted realm, this unknown territory, is the source of genuine abundance, and while it is impossible for any one of us to predict its precise pathways of operation, we *can* tap into it.

How? By giving.

When we're living a life of generosity, all sorts of value showers down upon us from that unnoticed, unseen place. We find a critical lead or make a crucial connection; a golden opportunity drops unexpectedly into our lap; we have some incalculably valuable thing come to us, not from the people or the places we were perhaps expecting or hoping for it to come from, but *from out of left field*.

The greatest gifts will come to you at moments and from places you least expect.

When you live generously and focus on creating value for others, great value will come to *you*, suddenly and unexpectedly—and in amounts far exceeding anything that anyone "owes" you.

This is what happens to Joe near the end of the story, and while Joe's story is fictional, what happens to him is not. We've seen it happen in real life hundreds of times, and we'll bet you have, too.

There is really nothing mystical about this. You cannot know from where these gifts will come simply because you cannot know exactly where your influence will have spread—but spread it has. You have planted so many seeds of goodwill, so many people know, like, and trust you and want you to succeed, that the world has become a benign context for your success. And while you cannot see its operation, there is indeed cause and effect. The cause is *giving*. And the effect? *Receiving*.

Dan Galbraith is a consultant in Greensburg, Pennsylvania, who provides support services to marketing professionals. Not long after attending one of Bob's live Go-Giver events in the spring of 2009, Dan wrote to say that he had undergone a fairly radical shift in how he viewed his business:

> It is remarkable how I look at my clients and colleagues now—and how that shift has generated unsolicited reciprocation from those same clients and colleagues. I am absolutely and totally swamped with business! I'm not sure if it is coincidence or not, but since I started applying these principles, business has been flowing in.

Of course, this sort of unexpected reward always *seems* coincidental—and never is. These things seem to come out of nowhere, but it would be more accurate to say that they come *out of everywhere*. We know only the minuscule 0.1 percent of the universe within which we live. These gifts come to us from the totality of the universe within which we are thoughtfully cradled, whether or not we are aware of it.

After twenty-five years of working in a high-stress corporate environment, Joe Vizi made the difficult decision to leave the corporate world. Today he and his wife, Renee, run Eco-Scrub, a Concord, Georgia–based family-owned carpet-cleaning business.

> About six months ago, we went to clean carpets for an elderly couple. They lived in a small two-bedroom assisted-living place about forty-five minutes away from our home. It was easy to see that they really

needed help: the Mrs. could not stand any straighter than at a ninety-degree bend at her waist, and the Mr. is legally blind.

Renee and I were there for a good three hours. It took us more time to organize their home than it did to do the actual carpet cleaning. We noticed some stacks of framed family pictures, but none were hanging on the walls.

Two weeks later Joe and Renee paid the couple another visit.

They were surprised to see us. We told them we'd come to help them hang their pictures. The elderly lady burst into tears. She said she couldn't believe someone would go out of their way like this for them.

"We can't pay you," she said, although we hastened to assure her that we were not expecting to be paid, "but what we can do is pray for you, and that we will."

Now, I'm not a deeply religious man, but I do believe that what goes around, comes around.

About two weeks later we attended an annual dinner for our local chamber of commerce—and to our surprise, we were awarded the county's Small Business of the Year! Based on what our clients tell us, winning that award has been responsible for about 35 percent of our new business in the past six months, putting its value in the thousands of dollars.

God, karma, whatever you believe is your choice— but it's clear to me that helping others is really for *your* benefit, and not only theirs. And it is great to sleep in peace every night.

There is a wonderful Yiddish expression: *Mensch tracht, un Gott lacht.* It means "Man plans, and God laughs."

As powerful as it is, goal setting is often overrated, because the targets *you* set are only half the story. Half, at most. It's good to have goals, but know this: no matter how big a goal you have, the universe—God, universal law, life itself, however your personal beliefs understand it—has a *bigger* goal for you. And the universe (God, universal law, life) is wiser than you are.

Wiser than all of us put together, actually.

Focus on creating value in the world around you and for the people around you, and the greatest opportunities will come to you in moments and from places you never expected.

30. Crisis

"'Cause I'll tell you, Gus, I'm already open to receive, honestly—I mean, I am really, really open!" [Joe] sighed and hunched back in his chair. "At least I thought I was. But it looks like the only thing I'm receiving is the short end of the stick."

These great gifts that come to you from unexpected places rarely arrive neatly wrapped and clearly marked, like lottery winnings in the mailbox or a new car in the driveway. Often they present themselves cloaked in the guise of *crisis*.

The person who asks the thorniest questions and voices the most difficult objections turns out to be one of your most loyal clients. The one who doesn't answer your emails and never buys your product gives you a referral who becomes the customer of a lifetime. The layoff that takes away your job steers you toward a new position that proves to be far more satisfying and lucrative.

It is often pointed out that the Chinese symbol for crisis (危機) is composed of two characters meaning *danger* and *opportunity*. This sense of crisis as a fork in the path is not unique to the East: the English word *crisis* comes from the Greek *krisis*, which means "choice."

During the Great Depression, a traveling salesman-turned-entrepreneur named Henry J. Kaiser built businesses that put tens of thousands of people back to work. Kaiser was so consistently fair to his employees that he earned the respect and admiration of trade unions—an especially impressive feat for the times. What is most intriguing about Kaiser's long and illustrious career is that his greatest achievements grew out of his response to failures, business closings, and other "catastrophes." On his deathbed Kaiser reiterated a saying that had guided him throughout his life:

Problems are simply opportunities in work clothes.

When you live a life of generosity, the world will bring you moments of shining good fortune—and they will often be decked out in tattered, oil-stained overalls.

This is why we often miss our greatest opportunities: we turn a deaf ear to the whispers of our intuition and fail to see through the work-clothes disguise. It's important to have a plan—but if we are too narrowly wedded to our own carefully blueprinted footpaths, we are more likely to miss the broader avenues that appear unexpectedly around the next bend in the trail.

Receptivity also means staying open to learning and to new ideas—and this takes courage.

It takes courage to step off the clearly marked map of our own plans and goals and out into the uncharted territory of the Unplanned.

Receptivity is a fragile thing, because to be receptive, you must leave yourself open. Keeping yourself genuinely open to a *yes* also means you expose yourself to a possible *no*. Having the courage to embrace an unexpected path also means embracing the risk that this path may (and sometimes *will*) lead nowhere—or nowhere good.

Perhaps this is the most challenging thing about being receptive: it means allowing yourself to be vulnerable.

The world can be a large and daunting place, at turns lonely and intimidating, brutal and perplexing. It is easy for us frail humans to feel jaded, burned, and embittered. Painful things happen. Deaths and betrayals, losses and failures, wounds and disappointments. These things are real. They've all happened to us, and surely they have happened to you, too. We are not suggesting you "put on a happy face" by denying the truth of your more painful life experiences, but that you embrace them.

These losses and failures have deep value. They have helped make you who you are, and they have given you greater depth, compassion, and understanding. The key is to embrace those experiences and, rather than letting them diminish your sense of trust in the world, let them *deepen* that trust. Yes, those things happened, and yet here you are, and a richer person for it.

Adversity changes us, but *how* it changes us is a *krisis*— a choice. Imagine losing your home, your family, your possessions, even your hope. For some, such an experience can lead to growth, wisdom, and great depth, while it leads others to become hardened and embittered.

There was a young man named Augustine whose mother believed in him. "Some day," she told her boy, "you will become a writer—and not just a writer, but a *great* writer."

The boy's life was happy until one day, six weeks after his high school graduation, while standing in the kitchen making her son's lunch, his mother suddenly fell dead.

Augustine joined the army, went to war, and upon his return began a career as an insurance salesman. His business did not do well, and he drifted deep into debt and drink. Eventually his wife took their daughter and left. Augustine roamed the country, sleeping in gutters, until he found himself one cold November day staring through a pawnshop window at a revolver with a twenty-nine-dollar price tag. He had thirty dollars in his pocket. "There's the answer to all my problems," the wretched man told himself. "I'll buy that gun, put it to my head, pull the trigger, and never have to face that miserable failure in the mirror again."

Krisis.

He chose not to buy the gun. Instead he wandered off and slipped into a library to stay warm . . . and there he began to read. And read. And read.

Soon he got another job in insurance, and as soon as he took his eyes off himself, he became very successful—and he began to write. Within a few years he wrote a little book that fulfilled his mother's prediction when it became an all-time best seller. The book is called *The Greatest Salesman in the World*, by Augustine "Og" Mandino.

Standing at that pawnshop window, Augustine confronted a fork in the path. The choice he made led to sales of some fifty million books, and changed millions of lives.

Not all of us will go through as much tragedy or pain as

Og Mandino, but surely we each face moments of hurt and difficulty in the pursuit of our dreams. The work clothes can be grimy indeed. Whether or not we see past them is up to us.

As Andy Dufresne says in that great film *The Shawshank Redemption*: "I guess it comes down to a simple choice, really. Get busy living, or get busy dying."

Danger; opportunity; choice.

31. Trust

I hate to sound so pragmatic and mundane, but what good is all that if it doesn't generate any wins in the marketplace? I could be a saint and starve to death!
                                                                            —JOE

Success emerges from the fabric of your influence in the world around you, and that fabric is woven from strands of trust. How do you get people to trust you? By being a trusting person.

Perhaps, as we suggested in the introduction, the biggest difference in the Go-Giver approach to sales has to do with the whole concept of *control*. Selling is not a process over which you can exercise absolute control, simply because it involves other people. You can control what you do; you cannot control what *they* do.

Here is the situation: the only way you can achieve financial success in sales is if other people do indeed buy your wares—and yet you have no real control over whether or not they do that.

Which means that sales itself is a process of putting your

livelihood—your life—in other people's hands. It is a business of becoming a professional truster of others.

Many salespeople do not grasp this. They still believe (despite all evidence to the contrary) that they can control the outcome; that if they just study hard enough, practice diligently enough, and become proficient enough, they will master the techniques that will put the levers of control into their hands and assure the outcome of their prospecting encounters.

But it's not so, because no matter how skilled, how practiced, how proficient you become, you cannot change this universal truth: *people will do what people will do*. All you can do is seek to serve, look for ways to create value—and trust.

And when you do, something remarkable happens: *others begin trusting you*.

"So you're saying I should trust *everyone*?" you might ask. "I don't want to be a cynic, but isn't that naïve? Not everyone is trustworthy!"

Living in a state of trust is not the same thing as being naïve. It's important to proceed with your eyes wide open to the practical realities of life. There are people who will try to take advantage of you, who are unscrupulous, who will seek to thwart your plans and subvert your success.

If you have a "healthy immune system," as Joe puts it, and keep your own attention focused on giving, you'll be far less likely to attract such people to you. "The disease is all around you, but you don't catch it." Still, that doesn't mean those people and circumstances don't exist.

But as you continue focusing on creating value for others and practice living in trust, something else remarkable happens: you become an ever better judge of character. Surprising, but true. Living in trust turns out to be virtually the opposite of being naïve: you become *more* perceptive, not less.

Why? Because you are practicing the Law of Receptivity. Being receptive means you are open, and being open means you increasingly see things as they are, not as you wish they were or fear they might be.

Just as being a trusting person does not mean being naïve, being receptive does not mean being passive. Being a Go-Giver doesn't mean you can't also be a *go-getter*.

If there is an opposite to Go-Giver, it is the person who lives on the constant lookout for how the world can serve *them*; the person who feels, "The world owes me, big time!"— you might say, a go-*taker*. And one trait go-takers universally share is a profound *lack* of trust—in anyone or anything.

Go-getters, on the other hand, take the initiative and make things happen, rather than waiting around hoping for things to go their way. Go-getters get things done. In fact, everyone we know who is a genuine Go-Giver is also a powerful go-getter.

A woman recently wrote us after reading *The Go-Giver*. She had been working hard to support herself and her sons, and things weren't going well. She said she now wanted to throw all her time and energy into a new idea to "make a living at giving." Her question:

Do I need to make a business plan to map out how I will make an income, or do I just dive right into the give part and take it on complete faith that money will appear from my actions?

Yes, we replied, you need to make a plan! Faith and pragmatic planning are not mutually exclusive. Both Ernesto and Nicole started out with very practical business models: selling hot dogs, designing and selling software. For that matter, so did Sam (selling insurance policies), Debra (selling houses), Claire (selling her graphic design and advertising services)—and indeed, so did everyone in the book.

Receiving is not something that simply happens on its own; it is a partnership between you and the world, and you each have your part to play. Living in trust means that having made your plan, you put it fully into action, investing it with excellence, consistency, attention, empathy, and appreciation.

Sales, as we mentioned earlier, is much like farming: you prepare the soil with care, you choose and plant the right seeds, you stay faithful in your watering, weeding, and cultivation—and God and nature do the rest. But you do have to plant and cultivate.

Create value; touch people's lives; build networks; be real; stay open.

Plant; trust; harvest.

ACKNOWLEDGMENTS

Writing a book is a thrilling experience—and a humbling one: you find out just how much you rely on the insight, patience, good humor, and generosity of all the people around you. We have been blessed to be surrounded by the best. Our deepest thanks and admiration go out:

To the multitude of participants in our Go-Giver community who have read *The Go-Giver*, followed the Go-Giver blog, and let us know how Pindar's principles of cooperative commerce have touched their lives;

To all those friends who provided vignettes and real-world examples from their own experiences to help breathe life into the ideas on these pages: Gilles Arbour, Simon Barrett, Heather Battaglia, Mark Beckford, Dan Galbraith, Dixie Gillaspie, Danielle Herb and Marianne St. Clair, Jim Hurlburt, Marie Jakubiak, Svetlana Kim, Annette Kraveck, Laura H., Og Mandino, Gilbert Melott, Terri Murphy, Bill Porter, Bea Salabi, James P. Smith, Arlin Sorensen, Gabe Strom, Sybil Temtchine, Brian Tomkins, Gary Vaynerchuk, Joe and Renee Vizi, Bradley Will, and Sean Woodruff;

To our eagle-eyed editor Adrienne Schultz, visionary publisher Adrian Zackheim, and the rest of the amazing team at Portfolio: Brooke Carey, Maureen Cole, Nick Owen, Will Weisser, and Courtney Young;

To Dan Clements, Jim Rohrbach, and Gill Wagner, for

reading the manuscript and offering insights and much-needed critique;

To screenwriter-director extraordinaire Fiona Ashe and Internet maven Kathy Zader for their unique talents and dedication;

To our stratospherically inspired and inspiring team at the McBride Literary Agency: Margret McBride, Donna DeGutis, Anne Bomke, and Faye Atchison, who are so much more than agents: ace editors, coaches, advisors, and most of all friends;

To our brilliant friend and resident promotional genius, Thom Scott, for helping transform *The Go-Giver* from an idea into a living, breathing global community;

To John's wife, partner, best friend, and better half, Ana Gabriel Mann, for her sweet and giving spirit;

And finally, to our parents, Mike and Myrna Burg and Alfred and Carolyn Mann—for giving us everything.